2nd Edition

Title Insurance
for Real Estate Professionals

Jeanine W. Johnson

This publication is designed to provide accurate and authoritative information in regard to the subject matter covered. It is sold with the understanding that the publisher is not engaged in rendering legal, accounting, or other professional service. If legal advice or other expert assistance is required, the services of a competent professional should be sought.

President: Mehul Patel
Executive Director of Product Development: Kate DeVivo
Managing Editor: Anne Huston
Managing Editor: Tony Peregrin
Development Editor: Megan Bacalao Virkler
Director of Production: Daniel Frey
Senior Managing Editor, Production: Jack Kiburz
Production Artist: Cepheus Edmondson
Creative Director: Lucy Jenkins
Vice President of Product Management: Dave Dufresne
Director of Product Management: Melissa Kleeman

© 2008 by Dearborn Financial Publishing, Inc.®

Published by Dearborn™ Real Estate Education
30 South Wacker Drive
Chicago, Illinois 60606-7481
(312) 836-4400
www.dearbornRE.com

All rights reserved. The text of this publication, or any part thereof, may not be reproduced in any manner whatsoever without written permission from the publisher.

Printed in the United States of America

11   12   13   10   9   8   7   6   5   4   3

ISBN-13: 978-1-4277-7886-4
ISBN-10:   1-4277-7886-8

contents

preface v
about the author v
acknowledgments v

Chapter 1 — The Basics of Title Insurance 1

Learning Objectives 1
Key Terms 1
What Do Title Insurance Companies Do? 1
What Do Title Insurance Companies Not Cover? 4
Title Insurance and Private Rights in Land 5
Three Areas Title Insurance Companies Examine for Risk 7
Summary 10
Case Study 10
Review Questions 11

Chapter 2 — The Business of Title Insurance 12

Learning Objectives 12
Key Terms 12
Title Assurance versus Title Insurance 12
Real Estate Settlement Procedures Act (RESPA) 14
Title Insurance Benefits and Helps Protect Everyone 15
Title Insurers versus Title Agents 18
Closing Liability versus Title Insurance 19
Summary 22
Case Study 22
Review Questions 24

Chapter 3 — Title Insurance Myths and Truths 25

Learning Objectives 25
Key Terms 25
Top Myths about Title Insurance 25
Summary 32
Case Study 33
Review Questions 34

Chapter 4 — How to Read Title Work Like a Title Professional 35

Learning Objectives 35
Key Terms 35
What Is the Title Commitment? 36
Parts of the Title Commitment 36
Reading Title Work—Title Exceptions Found on Nearly All Property 37
Understanding and Removing Exceptions 44
Types of Liens 47
Red Flag Title Problems 51
Summary 55
Case Study 55
Review Questions 57

Chapter 5 — Understanding Title Policies 58

Learning Objectives 58
Key Terms 58
Obtaining the Title Coverage You Want 58
The Two Primary Policy Types—Lender's and Owner's 60
ALTA Title Policies Have Six Elements 60
Summary 66
Case Study 66
Review Questions 68

Chapter 6 — Title Insurance Requires Professionals 69

Learning Objectives 69
Key Terms 69
Steps in the Title Insurance Process 69
Order Processors 70
Title Searchers 71
Title Examiners 72
Attorney/Closer/Closing Assistant 73
Recording Specialists 75
Other Title Company Personnel 75
Summary 76
Case Study 76
Review Questions 77

appendix 78
glossary 116
answer key 124

preface

Title insurance is a part of the real estate machine to which all real estate professionals belong. It is seriously misunderstood and is not given enough credit for its value to lenders, owners, agents, builders, and the economy at large.

Title companies close and insure billions of dollars each year in real estate transactions. They work with legal records, examining the old and helping create the new. Title companies deal daily with local, state, and federal laws, lender requirements, 20-page purchase agreements, and the stress of buyers and sellers. They work hard to make sure transactions go smoothly and accurately.

Title Insurance for Real Estate Professionals is designed for real estate agents, brokers, and lenders. First, it gives an appreciation of the title insurance industry that even veteran professionals often perceive as too complicated to understand. Second, it attempts to review familiar principles of real estate law—"the rights, title, and interests" professionals know—and relate them to the insuring of titles. Third, it is intended to allow a professional to correctly read and interpret both a residential title insurance commitment and a title policy. It will reinforce what professionals know, fill in some gaps, and provide new information that will be useful in your everyday business.

This book was prepared strictly as educational material. Information herein will vary somewhat from state to state and will change with each legislative session and as new case law is created. This material is deemed reliable as of the time printed, but it is not guaranteed and should not be considered as a substitute for advice from your title insurer.

■ About the Author

With more than 25 years of experience in the field of land titles, Jeanine W. Johnson has been a closer, title examiner, abstractor, and operations manager for both title agents and title underwriters. She has applied her knowledge to consulting and teaching for both the public and private sectors, working with county recorders, abstract and title insurance companies, law firms, lenders, surveyors, and many other professional organizations. Ms. Johnson has been an active member of the American Land Title Association, the National Association of Land Title Abstractors and Examiners, the Minnesota Land Title Association, and the Real Estate Educators Association.

■ Acknowledgments

The following persons provided valuable help in the creation of this book:

- Kathy Austen, Chicago Title Insurance Company
- Megan Bacalao Virkler, Dearborn Real Estate Education
- Kurt R. Johnson, JD
- James Maher, American Land Title Association

- Richard McCarthy, American Land Title Association
- Caitlin Ostrow, Dearborn Publishing
- Mike Solari-Stone, American School of Business
- Marie Spodek, DREI
- Steven J. Tierney, Stewart Title Guaranty Company
- Cindy Werner, Coldwell Banker Burnet
- Monica Williams, Coldwell Banker Burnet
- Judy Wolk, Charleston Trident Association of REALTORS®

chapter one

The Basics of Title Insurance

learning objectives

After completing this chapter, you will be able to

- discuss how title insurance indemnifies the insured;
- explain the "bundle of rights";
- summarize the components of real property covered under a title insurance policy;
- identify insurable interests in real estate; and
- list and discuss the four government rights.

■ Key Terms

actual notice	fixtures	life estate
bundle of rights	government rights	life tenant
constructive notice	improvements	real property
easement estate	indemnify	remainderman
encumbrances	insure	reversioner
fee simple absolute	leasehold estate	title
fee simple defeasible	liens	

■ What Do Title Insurance Companies Do?

When you buy fire insurance or flood insurance, it is unlikely that you believe your home will go up in flames or be flooded. But to protect yourself from the risk, you buy fire and flood insurance. With title insurance, you hope you will not be involved in fraud, forgery, identity theft, or dozens of other problems that could affect your title. You buy title insurance because you are not willing to take that risk on the biggest investment of your life.

A title company does a thorough search to determine title and other rights and interests that are vital to the owner of a property. It provides information on the status of title, showing such things as outstanding taxes, mortgages, easements, and restrictions. Purchasing an owner's title insurance policy provides protection for the owner's and lender's investments.

Title insurance companies **insure** title to real property, that is, they indemnify against loss or damage arising through defects in title. To **indemnify** means to make compensation for an incurred loss or damage. Thus, title insurance provides an insurance *policy*, which is a contractual liability wherein the insurer indemnifies a person against loss or damage. It is *not* a guarantee that title is as shown on the policy. It is *not* a guarantee that title is "good." It is *not* even a guarantee that you can maintain use, possession, or occupancy of the property. It *is* a monetary indemnity that the insured will receive compensation for loss or damage, up to the face amount of the title policy, if the title is not as shown on the policy.

Title refers to the rights of ownership in real property that are recognized and protected by law. These private rights fall under the general categories of

- use,
- possession,
- occupation,
- control,
- exclusion,
- disposition, and
- enjoyment.

In other words, title covers just about everything you can do to a piece of real estate.

> Discussion: List things an owner can do to a piece of real estate.

When a title policy covers a legal description such as "Lot 1, Block 6, Blackacre" it covers *all* of the real property components. **Real property** itself consists of the components to the land, including the surface, subsurface, air space, and rights that go with the land. (See Figure 1.1.)

Improvements to the land are also covered in a title policy. **Improvements** are those items attached to the land with the intent of being permanent, whether natural (trees, bushes, etc.) or artificial (houses, garages, driveways, etc.).

Fixtures are also insured under a title policy. **Fixtures** are items of personal property attached to the land or structure so that they legally become part of the real estate. Examples include heating, plumbing, and electrical fixtures.

There are two important exceptions to the fixtures rule. First, *trade fixtures* are articles typically installed by a tenant under the terms of a lease. The fixtures are generally for use in a trade or business. Examples of this are hair dryers and sinks in a beauty parlor, or booths and ovens in a restaurant. They are removable by the tenant before the lease expires and are not considered real estate.

Figure 1.1 | Real Property

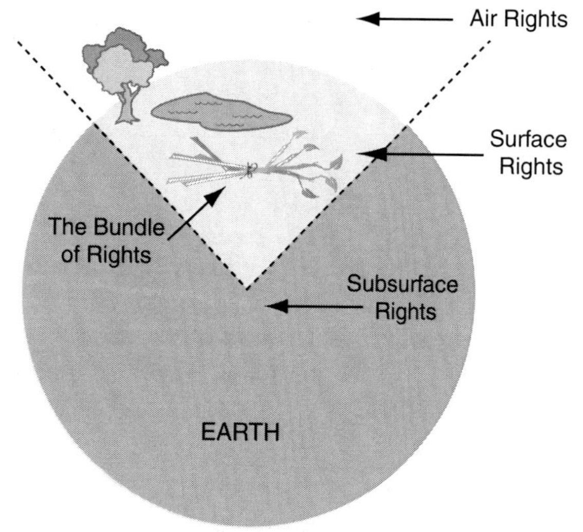

[Diagram showing Earth as a circle with a V-shape extending upward from the center. Labels: "Air Rights" pointing to top, "Surface Rights" pointing to the surface area, "Subsurface Rights" pointing below surface, "The Bundle of Rights" pointing to the apex, "EARTH" labeling the circle. Caption below: "Real Property"]

Second, *emblements*, or annual farm crops, are also generally an exception to the fixtures rule and can be sold separately from the land. A purchase agreement should specifically clarify disposition of these items.

Real property is generally sold or transferred by a deed, but it may be transferred by probate or court order (such as in a divorce, foreclosure, or tax sale) as well as by other means, such as adverse possession, eminent domain, or escheat.

> Discussion: Give examples from the room you are in of personal property. List examples of personal property that may have great value.

Personal property by definition includes everything that is not real property. Personal property is sold by a document called a "Bill of Sale" and is secured (mortgaged) by a Uniform Commercial Code (UCC) document known as a "financing statement." Personal property liens are filed in a special department called the "chattels" department, typically located in the local real estate recording office or in the office of the Secretary of State. Transfers and "mortgaging" of personal property do not show in the land records. On commercial properties, such as a hotel, restaurant, or farm, where significant amounts of personal property are being sold, a separate search is usually made for ownership of and liens on personal property. Title insurance generally does not insure personal property, although title companies may do searches for liens on personal property when requested, and endorsements can sometimes be negotiated to cover personal property.

Modular housing or mobile homes create an interesting problem for a title insurance company. Are they insuring it as real or personal property? The following guidelines are used to answer that question:

- To be mortgageable under FHLMC, FNMA, or GNMA rules, a modular home or mobile home must be permanently affixed with a "documented, engineered foundation."

- Different states have different statutes for transferring modular housing and mobile homes, but, generally, to be transferred as real estate the following must be present:
  - The assessing office should show the structure as part of the real estate for tax purposes.
  - The real estate tax statement should include the structure in its value. Mobile homes that are personal property may be taxed with personal property taxes.
  - Once a mobile home has been permanently attached, and when there has been a Certificate of Title issued for the mobile home (similar to a Certificate of Title for a car), the certificate must be turned into the state to be canceled.
  - Other specific requirements may be required in your state.

> Title insurance uses Endorsement Form 7 to the policy to specifically insure that modular or manufactured housing is real property. See Figure 1.2.

What Do Title Insurance Companies Not Cover?

Certain real estate rights always belong to the government. These so-called "government rights" are unattainable to an individual and are always exclusions to coverage under a title policy.

Government Rights in Real Property

Government rights in real property are exclusions to title coverage. Government has the following four categories of rights in real property:

1. *Police powers* (also known as *government powers*) occur at all levels of government (federal, state, and local). **Government rights** are designed to protect the public by creating laws and rules to assure the health, welfare, and safety

Figure 1.2 | ALTA Manufactured Housing Unit Endorsement 7

ALTA Manufactured Housing Unit Endorsement 7

ENDORSEMENT ATTACHED TO AND MADE A PART OF POLICY OF TITLE INSURANCE
SERIAL NUMBER _____
ISSUED BY
TITLE COMPANY
HEREIN CALLED THE COMPANY

Order No.:

The term "land" as defined in this policy includes the manufactured housing unit located on the land at Date of Policy.

This endorsement is made part of the policy and is subject to all of the terms and provisions thereof and of any prior endorsements thereto. Except to the extent expressly stated, it neither modifies any of the terms and provisions of the policy and any prior endorsements, nor does it extend the effective date of the policy and any prior endorsements, nor does it increase the face amount thereof.

Signed under seal for the Company, but this endorsement is to be valid only when it bears an authorized countersignature.

of the public. Police powers excluded from a title policy include such things as zoning ordinances.

2. *Eminent domain* is the legal right of the government to take land when "necessary for the public good," with "due process" of law, by providing "just" compensation. The common name for the process is also known as "condemnation." It is most commonly used when taking lands for public roads.

3. *Taxation* is the government's right to charge fees on property to gain revenue. They can take title to property if taxes are not paid.

Real estate taxes are always considered a "first lien" on the property because they have priority over all other liens. This means no notice has to be placed into the public record stating that there are real estate taxes due. The public is simply charged with knowing that any owner of real estate must pay real estate taxes or risk losing their land.

The government also reserves the right to collect federal and state taxes. While these are not real estate taxes, they must also be paid or an individual risks losing his or her property. However, these taxes are not "first liens" on the property because the liens attach only when a legal Notice of State Tax Lien or Federal Tax Lien has been recorded.

4. *Escheat* refers to the government's right to take real or personal property when a person dies, if he has no heirs and has left no will. Under the laws of intestate succession, it is very unlikely that a person will die with no heirs. Attorneys often talk about the "laughing heir rule," a situation where a fifth cousin six times removed is the last surviving heir of a wealthy tycoon. Upon the tycoon's death, the distant heir inherits everything, but, having never met the tycoon, the heir laughs all the way to the bank.

> To remember the four categories of government rights in real property, use the acronym PETE (**P**olice powers, **E**minent domain, **T**axation, **E**scheat).

Government rights exist in hierarchy (i.e., priority order). The federal government has the highest priority, followed by state, county, and municipal (city, village, etc.) government.

Generally, when the federal government passes a law, its decision will "trump" any laws created by state or local government. For example, because the federal government passed fair housing laws—prohibiting discrimination due to race, creed, religion, national origin, sexual orientation, marital status, familial status, or handicap—any law a state, county, or city passes in contradiction to the federal law would have no effect.

Or, when a state passes a law pertaining to the environmental control, any law a county or city passes in contradiction to the state law would have no effect.

There are many exceptions to federal law trumping state law. Certain rights, such as banking rights, insurance rights, and real estate and marital rights, are reserved to the individual states. This means laws pertaining to these items are made at a lower, more local level, and laws in these categories will vary from state to state.

> Because government rights are exclusions to title insurance, items such as zoning or building codes are not covered. However, when the government intends to exercise its rights, it files a "notice" in the public record. Title work discloses any such notice, so the buyer and lender are informed as to what government rights are being planned and the consequences.

■ Title Insurance and Private Rights in Land

Title is often discussed in terms of a **bundle of rights** (see Figure 1.3). Each right is a "stick" in the bundle. Owners of real estate have control over any rights or "sticks" that they have received from a previous owner. However, it is likely that they may not have received all of the rights to a piece of property because of outstanding encumbrances and liens.

Figure 1.3 | Bundle of Rights

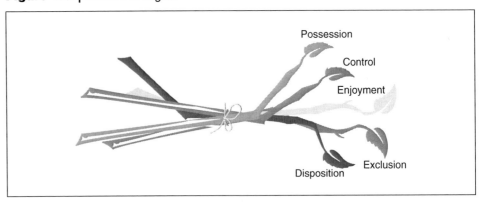

> An encumbrance is *anything* that may diminish the value of the property. Encumbrances may or may not be able to be released (e.g., restrictions or easements). Liens are a type of encumbrance that can be paid off and released.

Encumbrances include a wide variety of rights such as easements, restrictions, and mortgages that, once missing from the bundle, may or may not be obtainable to the owner or new buyer. For example, a new owner generally must make use of his or her property subject to the restrictions or easements on the property but may either pay off or assume the mortgage on the property.

Liens are a subset of encumbrances. Liens are security rights or money rights. Lien rights missing from the bundle, such as state or federal tax liens, attorney liens, or mortgage liens, may be returned to the bundle by simply paying off the lien. Liens are always removable by paying them off.

Over time, as there are more and more owners, and more and more uses of the land, possible rights, titles, and interests have multiplied, making the chain of title more complex. Remember, titles can be created by deed, will, inheritance, court order, or operation of law, and they are affected by both general and specific liens. All of these are parts of the ownership puzzle examined by the title company. Locating the chain of title and liens is a very specialized process, requiring a specialist in land titles called an **abstractor**.

Insurable Private Rights and Estates

Title insurance can insure almost any estate in real property—fee ownership, a life estate, a time-share, a leasehold estate, an easement estate, and so on. Some insurable estates are the following:

- **Fee simple absolute**, generally known as *fee*, or *fee title*, is the maximum *private* interest in land, subject to the rights of the government as described above. It is the most commonly insured type of title. However, there is also a **fee simple defeasible** estate, where title can be *defeated* by a restriction.

    For example, a deed states "this property is given to the city for use as a public park and in the event it is no longer used as a public park, it will revert, or forfeit to the heirs of the grantor." This property is generally unsalable and is certainly not mortgagable. This type of restriction would need to be removed in almost every instance.

- *Equitable interests* are those where a party has the absolute right to obtain title, such as a vendee under a contract for deed (or land contract) or an option agreement. Vendees' interests and optionees' interests are insurable.

- A **life estate** is used to provide ownership to real property for someone during his or her lifetime. Their ownership expires upon the person's death and is not transferable. The owner, called a **life tenant,** has fee for his or her life, but no inheritable rights. Disadvantages to this include the following: A life tenant cannot sell a fee interest. While the life tenant can lease the land, the lease will expire upon death of the life tenant. Because most lenders will not accept life estates as collateral, the life tenant consequently will not be able to mortgage the property. A **reversioner** is the giver of the life estate to whom the property reverts upon death of the life tenant. A **remainderman** is a specified third party to whom the property reverts upon death of the life tenant. A life estate can also be given *per autre vie*, or for the life of someone other than the life tenant. For example, a father dies, leaving a life estate to Tom, the caregiver of his son Ben, for Ben's life. Tom loses his rights upon Ben's death.

Discussion: When might someone want to use a life estate? Who has fee in a life estate? For how long does a life tenant hold title? How does one remove a life estate?

- A **leasehold estate** is the right of a tenant to possession of real estate during the term of a lease. While the lease is actually personal property, the interest is still an insurable interest for title insurance purposes. Leasehold estates are most often used with sales of cooperative units, where the fee owner is the cooperative association and the buyer holds a lease and stock in the association.

- An **easement estate** is the right to use a specific parcel of land, owned by another, for a specific purpose. Typical examples might include "a ten foot easement over the front lot line of Lot 1, Block 1, Blackacre, for telephone, cable, and electrical services," or "an easement for ingress and egress over the West 30 feet of Johnson Addition to reach Garcia Lake." Easements can add tremendous value to real estate and are commonly insured.

■ Three Areas Title Companies Examine for Risk

Title insurance companies are concerned with three legal areas that determine rights, title, and interests in land: constructive notice, actual notice, and rights that exist as a consequence of law. With careful examination, searching public records, physically inspecting the property, and asking questions, most rights can be determined. However, other interests such as unrecorded documents and fraud will not be found even with the most careful and competent examination. In order to mitigate or reduce potential losses, title companies investigate all three areas as carefully as possible.

Constructive Notice

Constructive notice means those rights shown by the public records. The law presumes a person knows information made available through the public recording system. Parties are presumed by law to have inspected the public records and to have knowledge of information in those records.

> Some liens, such as real estate taxes, are an exception to the recording rule and do not have to be recorded to affect title to the property. Many states also have exceptions to the recording rule for rights of contractors and subcontractors when improving the property.

Generally speaking, however, only documents that are properly recorded provide legal notice to the public of rights of ownership, mortgages, easements, restrictions, and so on. Properly recorded notice means the following:

- The documents are recorded in the correct public recording office and properly indexed.

- Documents filed in the wrong office have no legal effect.
- Real estate records are county-specific (or locale-specific)—that is, they only affect lands in the jurisdiction (usually county) in which the documents are filed. In some instances, the real estate recording office may be located in the city or parish. If you obtain a mortgage and want it to be enforceable, file it where the property is located! If you obtain a judgment against someone and want it to be enforceable against the debtor's property, you must file it in the county where the debtor owns property.

Constructive notice establishes the priority of a lien. The proverbial "race to the courthouse" means that the first person to record has legal title or rights over those filing later unless he or she had actual notice of the rights of the later filer.

Effective Date and Gap

There is most often a time gap between the time the closing happens and the time documents are sent for recording, are processed, and finally appear in the public records. This is known as the "gap" period. You will notice that the title commitment has an "effective date." The *effective date* is the date through which all documents can be located in the public records that affect title to the land. The effective date one sees on title work is a snapshot in time, as it reflects title as of that certain moment. The date may be almost current, or it may be weeks behind. The title company is very interested in what has happened to the property during this "gap" in time, as it impacts the title. Also, because closing does not occur for some days or weeks later, the title company will check the public record again at the time of closing to see if additional documents such as mortgages, divorce decrees, or liens have been recorded that might affect the title. During that time is it very possible people could have taken out another mortgage or had some kind of a lien filed that would affect title to the property.

It should be noted that the date of recording controls the priority of a document rather than the date shown on the document or the date notarized. For example, a mortgage for $150,000 was dated and notarized on January 2, and another mortgage for $5,000 was dated and notarized on February 28. If the $5,000 mortgage was recorded first, it would become the first mortgage, and the $150,000 mortgage would be in second position. This concept is known as "race to the courthouse."

Actual Notice

Actual notice is another key legal area that concerns title companies. One has actual notice when something can be observed, heard, or sensed. Therefore, title insurers mitigate, or lessen, their risks by investigating issues where they have actual notice. For example, if a title company received a second application for title insurance along with a purchase agreement on a piece of property, it would have actual notice of interests from the first and would want to clarify that the first purchase agreement had been cancelled.

By law, parties in possession (be it owners, renters, or a telephone company with a telephone pole on the property) give actual notice because everyone can see their possession. In order to investigate this right, the title company will often require an inspection, plat, or survey of the property. (See Appendix Figure 6.) They will be looking for such things as signs of actual notice—parties in possession, easements, encroachments, access, and survey issues. An inspector is given a checklist of things to look for and reports back to the title company.

In many states, parties who supply material or labor to a property have lien rights *without* recording any documents. They are an exception to the recording rule. In order to determine such rights, title company inspectors look for visible signs of new improvements, such as visible repairs to the property or new windows, and they check to determine if building materials have been delivered to a site.

Typical matters disclosed by inspection might also include overlaps, overhangs, misplaced boundary markers, violated restrictions, drainage ditches in use, party walls, joint driveways, encroachments, and visible signs of unrecorded easements such as power lines or fire hydrants.

Rights Existing as a Consequence of Law

These rights are often undeterminable, but they are as real as any other rights. These rights include numerous things, such as unrecorded documents, grantors being under legal age, fraud, forgeries, duress, insanities, incompetency, unknown heirs, undisclosed marriages, and identity theft. Unfortunately, these things happen every day. Title companies take these on as calculated risks. That is part of what a title company does and part of how title companies protect the public.

In order to mitigate (or lessen) their risks in these areas, the title company will take *affidavits*—legally sworn statements that are notarized and enforceable by law—from both the buyers and sellers asking pertinent information as to the status of title. The affidavit (see Appendix Figures 8 and 9) will ask such questions as the following:

- "What are your addresses for the previous (ten) years?" This question allows the company to compare addresses of buyers and sellers against those listed in judgments of record to see if the judgments *are* against them, or just against a name the same as, or similar to, the buyer's or seller's name. If the judgment is against someone with a similar name, the affidavit (often known as an Affidavit of Non-Identity or an Affidavit of Non-record Matter) will explain the name similarity and may be recorded to clear the problem.
- "Have you furnished any material or labor to the premises for the past (120 days) for which payment has not been made?" The answer to this question tells the title company if there are outstanding bills to be paid that could lead to mechanics' liens.
- "Are there any outstanding judgments or liens filed against you?"
- "Have you received any notices from a governmental agency that would affect the title?" This question looks for possible notices that the owner may have received, where no documents have yet been recorded.

All of these questions, and more, are designed for risk elimination. Should the buyer or seller lie on these affidavits, the title company has a cause of action against them and may sue for judgment to regain any money lost.

Title companies are also careful to ask for identification to avoid forgeries or fraud and to watch for signs of incompetency or duress that could affect the title.

> Discussion: Have you been involved in, or are you aware of, any illegal transfers of title that occurred or were attempted in your state?

Forged deeds in New York: Title insurance covers owners and lenders for losses due to forgery. A New York sales agent took only one day to tour a prosperous area, make a list of vacant properties, obtain copies of corresponding deeds, and file forged documents! In a short time, the sales agent had advertised the properties, entered into contracts with ready buyers, and quickly sold both houses and apartment buildings, taking in significant down payments.

Summary

Title companies use basic real estate principles to insure title to real estate. They insure the surface, subsurface, air space, and other rights that go with the land. In order to do so, they examine constructive notice, actual notice, and rights that exist as a consequence of law. They issue title work with an effective date, and when the transaction closes they again check the public record to see if additional documents have been filed that might affect title. They ask questions and take affidavits in order to determine all "rights missing from the bundle" and to issue as complete a title report as possible. They often obtain a survey or inspection and plat drawing. However, even with the most thorough and competent examination, title companies take risks due to such things as fraud, forgery, and unrecorded or misrecorded documents. The only way consumers can protect themselves from these unidentifiable items is with a title insurance policy.

case study

Charles is the owner of Blackacre. During his life, he gives a life estate to his sister Pam, who has been taking care of their disabled mother. The grant states that the life estate will terminate on the mother's death and the property will revert to Saint Andrews Church.

In this case study,

1. _____ is the life tenant.

2. _____ is the grantor.

3. _____ is the remainderman.

4. _____ would be the term used for Charles if the property returned in fee to Charles upon the mother's death.

5. Is a life estate an insurable estate? ____yes ____no

Review Questions

1. Why would a buyer or lender wish to purchase title insurance?
   a. To know the status of title
   b. To make sure unwanted liens are paid
   c. For protection
   d. All of the above

2. Title insurance is
   a. a promise that title is as shown on the policy.
   b. monetary indemnity that the insured will receive compensation for loss.
   c. a guarantee that you can maintain, use, possess, and occupy your property.
   d. a guarantee that title is "good."

3. Real property consists of certain elements that are bought, sold, mortgaged, leased, inherited, and so on, separately. These would NOT include
   a. easements.
   b. minerals.
   c. air rights.
   d. encroachments.

4. Chattels include which of the following items?
   a. Contracts
   b. Minerals
   c. Trees and landscaping
   d. Detached garages

5. Personal property is most often sold by a
   a. warranty deed.
   b. bill of sale.
   c. quitclaim deed.
   d. Uniform Commercial Code (UCC) document.

6. Emblements (crops) on a farm when attached to the land
   a. are part of the real estate.
   b. are personal property.
   c. should be clarified in a deed of sale.
   d. always belong to a tenant farmer.

7. Personal property is to a UCC what real property is to a
   a. mortgage.
   b. quitclaim deed.
   c. financing statement.
   d. bill of sale.

8. What are always considered a first lien on real estate?
   a. State taxes
   b. IRS taxes
   c. Government taxes
   d. Real estate taxes

9. Which refers to the government's right to take real or personal property when a person dies, if he or she has no heirs and has left no will?
   a. Eminent domain
   b. Police power
   c. Encroachment
   d. Escheat

10. Rights of the government generally exist in which order (first shown in series has highest priority)?
    a. State, county, federal, city
    b. County, federal, city, state
    c. Federal, city, county, state
    d. Federal, state, county, city

chapter two

The Business of Title Insurance

learning objectives

After completing this chapter, you will be able to

- describe the differences between title assurance and title insurance;
- discuss how title insurance benefits primary and secondary mortgage markets, buyers, sellers, and real estate agents;
- distinguish a title underwriter from a title agent and describe the roles of each; and
- discuss title liability and closing liability and describe how to protect clients from potential closing issues.

Key Terms

captive reinsurance
closing protection letter
coinsurance
defalcation
effective date
insured closing letter
insure over
reinsurance
secondary mortgage market
title agents
title assurance
title commitment
title insurance
title insurers/title underwriters
title policy

Title Assurance versus Title Insurance

Title assurance is a broad term that includes various forms of title information and evidence, including abstracts of title, attorney's opinions of title, Torrens certificates, land surveys, and title insurance.

Title insurance is a specific contractual obligation by an insurance company to reimburse the insured for any loss or damage resulting from erroneous or inaccurate representations of title as shown on the policy. It also insures legal access to the land, marketability of title, and insures against a host of undeterminable problems such as fraud, forgery, unknown heirs, defects in public records, and incompetent grantors.

Title insurance is the highest form of title assurance. It replaces reliance upon the work of individuals and substitutes corporate indemnity. It provides the most secure form of title assurance created to date. The American Land Title Association (ALTA) is the trade organization of companies dedicated to searching, reviewing, and insuring land titles to protect homebuyers and mortgage lenders who invest in real estate. ALTA title policies are the standard for the industry.

Alternative Products to Title Insurance

Many alternative products to title insurance have been proposed and introduced into the market. However, none of these alternative products provides protection for owners. Following are three of the alternative products:

1. *Casualty insurance products.* These promote elimination of the standard procedures of a title company. Casualty insurers believe there is no need to do a thorough search of the land records, obtain surveys, and so on. They suggest that in the event someone claims (after the closing) that there is a title problem, they should just fix the problem. There would, of course, be a charge pertaining to the title because some titles would need to be repaired. But they suggest the charge could be significantly less than a lender's title policy because so little work would be done investigating the title. They also suggest that any "high risk loans" would need title insurance because of potential losses and liability. And, of course, with minimal investigation of the title, loans could close almost immediately!

2. *Borrower's credit score.* Some lenders have suggested substituting a borrower's good credit for a lender's policy of title insurance. After all, if a lender can determine that it has a truly "good" borrower, one with a great credit score, who will undoubtedly make all payments on his or her mortgage, what are the chances the *lender* will suffer a title problem? After all, even with *no* title, if the lender is paid in full by the borrower, the lender has no problem. Again, there would still need to be a charge pertaining to title in those rare instances where a lender would have to repair the title because they needed to take the property in a foreclosure, and it had a bad title.

3. *Owner and encumbrance report.* One large bank made mortgage money available using "owner and encumbrance" (O&E) reports that provided information on the last deed of record, and other cursory information, without a complete title search. (Items such as easements and restrictions, for example, are not listed on an owner and encumbrance report.) While an O&E report provides some minimal assurance to the bank, no one is looking out for the interests or concerns of the borrower or owner here.

There has been significant litigation with some of these alternative products. In many states, courts have found alternative title products to constitute a bogus form of title insurance, contrary to the best interests of the public, and the courts have banned the products.

These alternative products offer no protection for buyers or owners of property. They do not even purport to give basic protection as to ownership or liens or encumbrances of record, let alone protection against fraud, forgery, identity theft, or other potential problems. These "advanced, alternative" plans ignore the key role that title insurance plays in a transaction, a role that has served both the mortgage market and owners well over decades for a reasonable fee.

There are many misunderstandings surrounding title insurance, but its role is vital to protecting the interests of the public. It protects buyers, sellers, lenders, and real estate agents. In addition, it plays a crucial role, economically, by providing a mechanism for the sale of mortgages to the secondary market, helping to give the United States the highest home ownership rates in the world.

Reinsurance and Coinsurance

Because of the potentially enormous monetary risk involved in large real estate projects like the Twin Towers or Mall of America, underwriters share risks among several companies by use of **reinsurance** or **coinsurance**. When reinsurance is used, the originating underwriter assumes liability for the whole risk. However, as soon as the transaction is closed, it "cedes off" a portion of the remaining risk to one or more reinsurers. The various reinsurers are paid a portion of the premium to assume their respective portion of the risk (the first $5 million, the second $5 million, etc.). When coinsurance is used, the risk is divided equally among two or more underwriters at the onset of the transaction, and each picks up their respective half, one-third, etc., of any losses due to a claim.

Real Estate Settlement Procedures Act (RESPA)

Among the many laws that govern title insurers and agents is RESPA, which specifically does not allow kickbacks in a real estate transaction. Under *Sec. 2607. Prohibition against kickbacks and unearned fees* of RESPA, it stipulates that

> "No person shall give and no person shall accept any fee, kickback, or thing of value pursuant to any agreement or understanding, oral or otherwise, that business incident to or a part of a real estate settlement service involving a federally related mortgage loan shall be referred to any person." RESPA also stipulates that "the Secretary, the Attorney General of any State, or the insurance commissioner of any State may bring an action to enjoin violations…"

This area of law enforcement has been very active for legislators and regulators over the past few years.

Illegal Use of Captive Reinsurance

Recently, some title underwriters have illegally captured business by returning a portion of the premium to customers through use of captive reinsurance. The underwriter would reinsure 50 percent of the risk with a title agent created and owned by real estate agents, lenders, and homebuilders. In these illegal reinsurance deals, it was determined that the insurer was overpaying for the reinsurance, and, in effect, giving a kickback to the customer for the business. For complete information on the scheme, see a detailed report at *www.naic.org/documents/govt_rel_issues_title_testimony_0604_toll.pdf*.

Illegal sham affiliated business arrangements. The other indirect form of kickback that state regulators and HUD are seeing across nearly all states is illegitimate or "sham" affiliated business arrangements. Affiliated business arrangements (AfBAs) are ownership arrangements between and among title insurance entities and lenders, homebuilders, real estate agents, and so on. Affiliated business arrangements are not inherently bad and offer consumers the convenience of one-stop shopping. However, some underwriters have sanctioned sham affiliated business title arrangements to control more business. Government entities have determined that title agents are sham operations by exposing fake title agents with no staff, the same address listed for many agencies, having little or no capital in the business, and companies where all title services were contracted out to another title agency or the underwriter. Regulators concluded that the only purpose for creating these entities was to construct vehicles to provide kickbacks to the real estate agents, builders, and mortgage brokers who owned the businesses. Accordingly, these entities are now being shut down. A good example of the types of affiliated business arrangements examined for sham operations can be found on the Colorado insurance Web site at *www.dora.state.co.us/insurance*.

■ Title Insurance Benefits and Helps Protect Everyone

When title insurance is properly created, lenders (both primary and secondary markets), buyers, sellers, and real estate agents all benefit from the title insurance product.

Protecting the Lender

Mortgage money is funded by two sources, the primary and secondary mortgage markets. We normally think of mortgage money in relation to the primary mortgage market, consisting of the mortgage lenders who *originate* the loans directly. These are generally banks, mortgage bankers, savings banks, savings associations, mortgage brokers, commercial banks, and so on. It is where we think to go to get a mortgage loan.

In order for primary mortgage lenders to have an abundant supply of money, they use the **secondary mortgage market.** The secondary mortgage market buys mortgages from the primary market, giving them more money to lend. The secondary market then packages and sells "securities" that are secured or backed by pools of mortgages, on the national market. Individual investors can buy the securities that supply a constant source of money for housing.

In order to provide confidence in the title to a pool of properties, a system was needed to cope with the variations in laws among the 50 states and standardize the quality of title assurance received. To meet this need, title companies created title policies with the following four universal requirements to describe what's acceptable and what's not acceptable in all parts of the country:

1. Title policies indemnify the lender against loss due to a bad title. After all, would you buy a mortgage not knowing if it is legitimate?
2. Title insurance companies use standardized forms that have been created through the joint efforts of the American Land Title Association (ALTA) and the mortgage banking industry and approved by FNMA, FHLMC, and GNMA. As much as possible, these policy forms are uniform between states. This uniformity helps simplify and facilitate mortgage lending both locally and across state lines, facilitating the sale of pools of mortgages. (Some states, such as Texas, have state mandated forms rather than the more typical ALTA forms. Iowa uses a system of abstracting, title opinions, and a title guaranty certificate issued by a division of the Iowa Finance Authority. Iowa is the only state where the sale of title insurance is prohibited.)
3. Title insurance homogenizes state laws and title assurances into a single system understandable to lenders and describes both what kind of title the lender is getting and what kind of title the buyer is getting.

4. Title policies help home ownership. Title insurance created a mechanism to help fund the largest percentage of home ownership in the world. For decades, Fannie Mae, Freddie Mac, and Ginnie Mae have both recognized and required title insurance as essential in protecting the reliability of mortgages made in the primary and secondary markets.

Protecting the Homeowner's Investment

Owners' policies provide comprehensive coverage by protecting the buyers' equity in the purchase of their homes. If an owner's policy is not purchased, they put their entire investment at risk.

Owners' policies are significantly different from lenders' policies. A homeowner needs to protect his or her investment with an owner's policy, separate from the lender's policy, for the following reasons:

- A lender's policy covers only the remaining loan balance, decreasing in time as the loan is paid down.
- A lender's policy is paid only when the lender has an actual loss. Therefore, even though there might be a complete failure of title, if the owner has paid the loan in full, the *lender* would have no loss and the title company would have no claim. Consequently, an owner cannot rely on a lender's policy to resolve a title problem.
- Lenders' policies are readily assignable, and, in fact, they usually specify the insured as "ABC Bank, its successors and assigns, as their interests may appear." An owner's policy is not assignable. The lender's policy is assignable because it obtains its lien rights against the title at the time the mortgage is recorded. When a first mortgage lender assigns its rights, for example, the rank of the first mortgage in the chain of title does not change. Even though the owner may have put on a second or third mortgage, those liens would have been recorded after the first mortgage and would be subordinate, or junior, to the first mortgage.
- Owners' policies are not assignable. When the new buyer comes along, there is a transfer in title. The new buyers take their position in the chain of title upon filing of the new deed. Sellers may have judgments filed against them, have taken out several mortgages, and so on, all since the seller has purchased the property. These would precede the rights of the new buyers in the chain of title. Therefore, new research will have to be done and a new policy issued. Buyers may also have state tax liens, federal tax liens, or judgment liens filed against them that would affect title to the property they are buying. These would need to be cleared before the title company would issue a title policy free of the buyer liens.

Owners' policies are written to cover the full sale price of the property. Coverage lasts as long as the owners, or their heirs, have title and persists even after the property sells. Consider Freddy and Frankie Fitzgerald, who bought a home from an estate five years ago. When they bought, a probate deed was provided by the seller's personal representative. They purchased an owner's policy that covers them from any loss due to title problems existing at the time they acquired title (whether bogus or not) and for claims against title after they sell. Three years later, Freddy and Frankie Fitzgerald sell by a warranty deed three years later to Billy and Bobby Byers, husband and wife. The Byers assume the Fitzgeralds' loan. Billy and Bobby are now refinancing and have just been notified of a title problem. An additional heir has shown up, claiming he has an interest. Even though Freddy and Frankie are out of title, they gave a warranty deed, assuring that title was

---

ALTA states an estimated 40 percent of U.S. homeowners, representing 48.8 million homes, do not have an owner's policy of title insurance to protect their investment. (ALTA press release, September 27, 2004, www.alta.org/press/release.cfm?newsID=2171) For lack of a small one-time premium, they are putting themselves at great risk on what is likely to be the biggest investment of their lives.

good. Because their owner's policy covers their warranties under the deed, the Fitzgeralds' policy will still handle the claim for the Byers and the Fitzgeralds.

In some regions of the country, it is customary for the seller to provide an owner's policy for the buyer. In other parts of the country, the owner purchases their own. By providing the buyer an owner's policy, the seller, buyer, and real estate agent will not have to worry about future liability for title problems.

Protecting the Real Estate Agent

While owners and lenders receive actual policies, title insurance also protects real estate agents in the following ways:

- Sellers who have previously purchased title policies are almost always assured that their transaction will go through smoothly when they come to closing.
- Real estate agents are assured they will not be embroiled in messy title problems, thus dealing with unhappy customers because of a title claim. After all, who will the clients blame if a title problem comes up and they haven't purchased an owner's policy?
- Title companies work to speed the purchasing process, so the transaction can move faster and more smoothly for buyers, sellers, and agents.
- Title companies also provide access to a variety of title professionals who are readily available to the real estate agent or broker to resolve problems or offer possible solutions to title issues.

Never tell buyers they do not need an owner's policy. If a real estate agent tells his or her buyer that an owner's policy is not necessary, that agent is putting himself or herself at risk. Should the buyer have a title problem after closing, he or she may sue the agent for bad representation and loss of any equity (not to mention anguish, pain, and suffering, etc.).

Real estate professionals must recognize that title companies "insure over" problems or "provide affirmative coverage" for lenders that they may not insure over for owners. One cannot assume that because the lender has a policy, the buyer's title must be okay. Title companies regularly "insure over" problems for "lenders' purposes only." *Insure over* means that if there is a recognized title problem, the title company may add a special endorsement to guaranty against loss or damage.

For example, let us say there is a small encroachment of a home onto a large easement. The new buyer is providing a large down payment, creating significant equity in the property. In this instance, the title company will likely "insure over" the problem by stating it will "guarantee the lender against any loss or damage to the property due to the exercise of the easement holder." *This does not make the problem go away, but it will allow the lender to sell the loan to the secondary market, and therefore, the lender can fund the transaction to close.*

The endorsement in this example, however, did *not* cover the owner. Moreover, the next buyer may question the marketability of title or the possible need to remove the building. Or, worse yet, the utility company may determine that the problem with the electric line actually lies underneath the structure, and may require its removal.

Insuring over a problem for an owner would have to be negotiated separately, but it is quite often available by request. As most homeowners are not aware this coverage is available, they don't ask for it. A good real estate agent, or title agent, can be a hero by asking for coverage for the owner's policy.

Important: A "Notice of Title Defect" is a standard form that should be provided to the borrower/owner to explain whenever there is an unresolved title problem that the title company is "insuring over." This form outlines the problem and informs the owner of the title issue. With or without an owner's policy, owners should never be left in the dark about any title issue. Special attention should be paid to the Notice of Title Defect form so that owners understand there are specific title risks on the property have been identified.

A "Notice of Availability of Owner's Title Insurance" is also an ALTA standard form (see Appendix Figure 1). It should generally be presented at closing, explaining to the buyers that a mortgage policy is being issued on behalf of their lender, but that the policy does not protect the owner unless they purchase a separate owner's policy. In some states this is a requirement. If the policy is purchased at a later date, the cost will be significantly more, because the interim time frame will have to be checked for changes in the chain of title, liens, and so on.

Title Insurers versus Title Agents

Title insurance policies are written in 49 states and many foreign countries. (All states but Iowa use title insurance. While Iowa state law dictates that title insurance cannot be written within the state, title insurance on Iowa property is frequently written outside the state.) There are thousands of title insurance companies in the United States. There are only a handful of title insurance underwriters—most title companies are agents for title underwriters. The term "title company" is used generically, referring to either a title insurer, also known as a title underwriter, or a title insurance agent. When the distinction is important, we will specify title underwriter or title agent.

Title insurers aka **title underwriters** actually assume title risks. Title underwriters are required to take a portion of each premium dollar and set it aside to pay claims. Title insurers are heavily regulated by state law. They are held to strict requirements as to how much money must be maintained for known claims and for *statutory premium reserves* (SPR), the term generally used for the state-mandated pool of money that a title insurer must have available to pay title claims. Less than ten title underwriters dominate the entire U.S. market, according to U.S. Census Bureau data (*www.census.gov*). Title insurance is also written around the world.

In order to sell more title insurance, title underwriters sell their policies through **title agents.** There are thousands of title agents in the United States. The title agent is an independent contractor for an underwriter (or underwriters) and "writes" the same policies as the underwriter. The title agents are often real estate attorneys or affiliated business arrangements (AfBAs), that is, entities associated with real estate companies, lenders, or builders as sister companies. The Real Estate Settlement Procedures Act (RESPA) has many legal guidelines as to how title agencies and title underwriters must act and disclose relationships.

Title underwriters often directly compete with their title agents, but financial strengths between underwriters and agents differ significantly. Title insurers have far superior financial strength. When a title claim occurs, the title agent turns the title claim over to the title underwriter who attempts to resolve the problem or pays the claim. It is important to note that unless an "insured closing letter" is given by the title underwriter, there is no title coverage for the handling of funds and no coverage for any issues related to closing when a title agent closes the transaction. (This will be discussed in further detail later in this course.)

Documentation—The Title Commitment or Binder

Prior to a policy being issued, a preliminary **title commitment** (also known as a title binder) is prepared, showing the status of title. This preliminary commitment informs parties of the status of the title, as of a certain date, called the **effective date**, and often will list requirements to be met in order to properly insure title. While there is some liability for the title company when issuing a commitment to insure, the title company does not actually take on liability until the closing has occurred and the premium is paid for the policy.

Documentation—The Title Policy

The **title policy** is the actual document that creates a liability on behalf of the title underwriter. It sets forth the terms and conditions of coverage, who is insured, the face amount of the policy, and the exceptions to coverage. The consideration paid for this insurance coverage is called the *premium*. The changes or modifications to the policy are accomplished by important documents called *endorsements*. Endorsements have a significant impact on title policies by providing additional coverage, and there can be dozens of endorsements issued, depending on the complexity of the transaction. For example, a shopping mall may need special endorsements for zoning rights, easements may need to be covered for access to the mall, etc.

■ Closing Liability versus Title Insurance

Title insurance companies handle billions of dollars in real estate closings every year. Closings also deal with the emotional stress of buyers and sellers, carry out lengthy purchase agreements, careful drafting of legal documents, and handling detailed instructions from the lender, along with the handling of HUD-1 closing statements and good funds.

Over recent years, title companies, attorney agents, and affiliated business arrangement title agents have taken on greater and greater roles in the area of closing. Over the past years, these closings have become more and more complicated. New types of loans—variable-rate, adjustable-rate, balloon, growing equity, interest-only, construction financing, reverse-annuity, and others—have moved into the market. These complex documents must be explained to the borrowers, which can be a very difficult task. Particularly evident is the lack of understanding of these documents in the real world, where foreclosures have run rampant the last years as the reality of the documents hits home.

New local and federal legislation related to the subprime market and poor quality loans that lenders are making will make closings even more difficult by requiring additional documentation in the future.

The complications of closing also include dealing with heavy legislation pertaining to federal laws such as the Patriot Act, truth-in-lending (TIL) laws, RESPA, and the Gramm-Leach Bliley Act (GLBA), which deals with privacy. In addition, at closing, fees for taxes, assessments, recording of documents, paying off old mortgages, judgments and liens, and a host of other monetary issues must be handled.

Independent "signing agents," a fairly new phenomenon in the United States, are unknowns in closing. Signing agents typically go to a home, bringing the documents with them for closing, and are frequently used in "signing" refinance transactions. Some signing agents see themselves strictly as notaries public, who witness signatures with no responsibility for explaining documents. They merely verify the identity of the signers. Other signing agents are very knowledgeable about the documents and may thoroughly explain them—but do they have errors and omissions coverage? If an error is made, who is responsible? Lenders are being sued because borrowers do not understand their mortgages.

While title insurers work hard to assure transactions go smoothly and accurately, the task becomes more difficult each day, and the risk of making a closing mistake is great. In the author's experience, at any moment, virtually all closers have mistakes that need to be resolved after closing.

Closing Liability

Title insurance policies legally indemnify the insured against *title* issues. They do *not* cover lenders or owners against numerous *closing* risks or errors. Therefore, a large monetary loss could occur due to closing problems. Closing losses can occur for many reasons; for example, a closer

- does not properly follow the closing instructions of a lender;
- does not properly follow the requirements of a purchase agreement;
- does not properly follow the requirements of title work;
- fails to collect all proper documentation;
- receives fraudulent documents;
- fails to properly pay off mortgages, taxes, assessments, or liens;
- has a **defalcation** (i.e., illegally diverts or steals funds), a title company's worst nightmare;
- has dishonest or fraudulent employees;
- does not properly record documents; or
- accepts "bad" funds (e.g., a check from the lender or purchaser is returned because of insufficient funds).

Again, a title insurance policy does not cover these closing issues per se because they are not *title* problems.

However, while the policy may not cover closing issues, some of these items, such as failure to pay liens, will likely become title problems with title insurance liability.

Closing companies generally bear their own respective risk and liability for closing problems. Make sure you know who is closing your transaction!

Title Insurance Agents Carry Some Liability Coverage for Closings

While title companies almost always maintain errors and omissions insurance for mistakes and bond employees who handle significant amounts of money, these precautions may not be adequate because of the very large sums of money handled in real estate transactions over a period of time. Even a very small title agent will handle tens of millions of dollars monthly in closings, and it is not unusual for a large agent to handle a billion dollars of closings in a single year. They generally do not carry enough errors and omissions insurance for the potential losses.

As a real estate agent, be careful to know the companies you are dealing with in terms of their solvency and how they are able to guarantee handling of significant sums of money. Considering that the size of a real estate transaction is frequently hundreds of thousands of dollars, even a single closing loss could be devastating to a title agency and the consumer. If the real estate agent has recommended the title company, he or she will likely be embroiled in a serious lawsuit.

Unfortunately, with the heavy volume of real estate business done between 2000 and 2006, many new, inexperienced title agents, including affiliated business arrangements, entered the business of insuring titles and closing loans in that period. With the volume of business available, title underwriters signed up many new agents. They are now paying the price. A number of these title agencies have gone out of business. For some, the handling of millions of dollars was just too much temptation. A number of these agents have caused tremendous financial pain to underwriters, as they absconded or misused customer's funds, did not pay off mortgages, forged releases, or did not record critical documents.

> Discussion: Print out, from a search engine like Google, several articles on title insurance fraud, mortgage fraud, or real estate fraud in your local market and discuss.

Here is a case in point. Like Kind Exchange was a 1031 exchange company specializing in the trading of real estate to defer capital gains taxes. A few years ago a restaurant owner sold his restaurant for $375,000, facing a capital gains tax if he didn't reinvest it into a new property. Under the advisement of his real estate agent, he turned the sale proceeds over to a title agent, Like Kind Exchange, while searching for a replacement property. He also paid Like Kind $900 up front to handle the exchange. Several months later, when the restaurant owner went to close on the exchange property, he found out that Like Kind Exchange no longer had his $375,000. In fact, Like Kind Exchange had filed for bankruptcy just a few days before the closing. According to the newspapers, the owner of Like Kind had "borrowed" the funds from the trust account to invest in the stock market right before its crash. ("Firm's Sheltered Money Disappears," *St. Paul Pioneer Press*, May 10, 2000.)

Closing Protection Letters

So how do consumers protect themselves against closing problems? Because many agents do not have deep enough pockets to sustain even a single transaction loss, lenders have looked to title insurance underwriters to take on that risk, requiring a document called a **closing protection letter** (see Appendix Figure 5) also known, in some parts of the country, as an **insured closing letter**.

Underwriters routinely provide closing protection letters to lenders. A closing protection letter is also available to any party to the transaction who gives instructions (e.g., the buyer or seller in a purchase agreement) and deposits funds or documents with the title company. But, the public at large is generally unaware of this protection and does not request it. Upon giving a closing protection letter, the title underwriter assumes the risk, insuring that it will reimburse the lender or owner for actual loss incurred in connection with the closing. Real estate agents can be champions with their customers by making sure their customers have an insured closing letter from the underwriter when closing with a title agent. A knowledgeable agent will protect his or her buyer (and himself or herself!) by requiring a closing protection letter.

■ Summary

Title insurance is a specific contractual obligation by an insurance company to reimburse the insured for any losses resulting from erroneous or inaccurate representations of title as shown on the policy. It also insures legal access to the land, marketability of title, and insures against a host of undeterminable problems such as fraud and forgery; undue influence; duress; incompetency; incapacity; impersonation; documents not properly filed, recorded, or indexed in the public records; encroachments; and much more.

Title insurance benefits lenders and the secondary market by describing what's acceptable and what's not acceptable in all parts of the country. Title insurance helps lenders cope with the variations in laws among the 50 states, and assists in sales to the secondary market. Owners' policies of title insurance provide comprehensive coverage by protecting buyers' equity in the purchase of their homes. Title insurance also helps real estate agents by making transactions go quicker, more smoothly, and preventing messy title problems with the help of title professionals. This makes for happier customers.

It should be noted that title insurers, not agents, actually assume title risks, setting aside a portion of each premium dollar to pay claims. Title policies only indemnify against *title issues*; they do not cover *closing* issues or errors. In order to cover that risk, the seller, buyer or lender needs a document called a closing protection letter. With closing protection letters from the title underwriter, the buyer and lender can be protected from fraud, dishonesty, or negligence in handling money and documents.

case study

Susan Alda bought a $239,000 home using Tom Smith, a local real estate agent. With guidance from her agent, she took a loan with the Midwest Loan Company and closed with the Acme Title Insurance Agency. She was required to buy a lender's title policy by the mortgage company, and at the agent's suggestion, she also purchased an owner's policy.

Six months after closing, Susan had a knock at her door. The sheriff told her that he was serving her with foreclosure papers from an unknown mortgage company. Susan called Tom, who assured her that it must be some type of mistake. Tom said he would contact the unknown lender and find out what was happening. In talking to the lender, Tom found out that the sellers' mortgage had never been paid off. Tom called the Acme Title Insurance Agency, who checked their records, said the loan was paid, and that the check had cleared. Acme called the lender, who assured them the loan was not paid. When Acme inquired about the cleared check, they were told that the check was applied to another loan number, per instructions. When Acme inquired as to how to clear up the matter, they were told that the full loan amount was due, plus six months worth of interest, and $3,600.00 in foreclosure costs, for a total due of $236,583.43.

1. In this case study, who is responsible to clear the closing error?
    a. Tom Smith, the agent, for choosing the Acme Title Insurance Company
    b. Midwest Loan Company, for using Acme
    c. Acme Title Insurance Company, for listing the wrong loan number
    d. Acme Title Insurance Company's title underwriter

2. As Susan's real estate agent, how could Tom have best helped Susan financially protect against closing mistakes?
    a. By closing at another title company
    b. By checking to see if the closer had errors and omissions insurance
    c. By checking to see if Acme bonded their closers
    d. By requesting a closing protection letter

Review Questions

1. Title assurance does NOT include which of the following?
   a. Attorney's opinion of title
   b. An unsigned deed
   c. Title insurance
   d. Land surveys

2. Title insurance also protects real estate agents by
   a. providing access to professionals to help resolve title problems.
   b. giving errors and omissions coverage to agents.
   c. providing title policies for lenders.
   d. handling large sums of money.

3. Title policies legally indemnify the insured against
   a. title issues.
   b. closing issues.
   c. title and closing issues.
   d. loss of the property.

4. Title agents maintain errors and omissions insurance for mistakes and for employees who handle large sums of money, title agents use a
   a. bond.
   b. insurance policy.
   c. cover statement.
   d. self-insurance account.

5. Mortgage money is funded by
   a. mortgage lenders and banks.
   b. mortgage lenders and mortgage brokers.
   c. FNMA, FHLMC, VA, and FHA.
   d. the primary market and the secondary market.

6. Which originate(s) loans directly to the consumer?
   a. Government entities
   b. The Federal Reserve Board
   c. The primary market
   d. The secondary market

7. Title companies meet the needs of the secondary market by
   a. indemnifying the lender against losses due to title problems.
   b. standardizing titles assurances across the country.
   c. creating a mechanism to assist the secondary market to securitize mortgages.
   d. All of the above

8. Prior to issuing a policy, the title company prepares a title binder or a(n)
   a. commitment.
   b. policy.
   c. endorsement.
   d. premium.

9. An insured closing letter does NOT assume risk for failure of the
   a. closing agent to comply with closing instructions.
   b. banks through which funds are drawn to be solvent.
   c. closing agent to collect "good" funds (a check bounces).
   d. closing agent to obtain necessary documents.

10. The term *defalcation* refers to the fact that
    a. title policies do not cover closing issues.
    b. the title policy is in error and has a claim.
    c. legal documents were not properly collected.
    d. funds have been stolen.

chapter three

Title Insurance Myths and Truths

learning objectives

After completing this chapter, you will be able to

- identify and dispel common myths about title insurance;
- describe why title insurance is a riskier business than in the past;
- discuss how title insurance is a risk elimination rather than a risk assumption business; and
- identify key claims issues in the title industry.

■ Key Terms

risk assumption   risk elimination

■ Top Myths about Title Insurance

> The most common misconception about title insurance is that it *guarantees* good title. It does *not* guarantee good title.

Discussed below are some of the most common myths, or misconceptions, about title insurance that real estate professionals should be aware of in order to help their clients make informed decisions about the optional purchase of an owner's policy of title insurance.

Myth 1—Title Insurance Is a Guarantee of Good Title

Many believe that an owner's title policy will assure they can't lose their home. That is wrong; even with a title policy everyone is susceptible to title losses, including loss of possession of the real estate. Fortunately, that rarely happens.

Truth. Title insurance *indemnifies* the insured when they have a loss because of covered defects, liens, or encumbrances that were not disclosed but existed on the date of the policy; the title company will either defend title and make it good or compensate the insured for the loss, up to the face amount of the policy.

Title insurance *cannot* and *does not* guarantee that a person can retain physical possession of property under any circumstances, but it can and does assume the monetary risk both for defending claims against title and for monetary loss. Even the best title examination cannot detect fraud or a forged signature on a document, or that a legally binding, but unrecorded, document does not exist. False impersonation of the true owner; forged deeds, releases, or wills; deeds by persons supposedly single, but in fact married; and unpaid estate, inheritance, gift, or other taxes are just a few examples of common claims. That is why people buy it.

Myth 2—A Lender's Title Insurance Policy Benefits the Owner

When a lender's title insurance policy is issued, many believe that title *must* be good, or the title company would not insure it. Therefore the buyer thinks he or she does not need an owner's policy.

Truth. A lender's policy benefits the lender only. It holds its value, increases in value, or decreases in value, depending on the terms of the mortgage. The policy amount is set to match the remaining balance on the mortgage. However, a lender's policy does not cover any of the owner's equity in the property, and covers the lender only when the lender has a title loss. Let's say there is an undiscovered title problem, and the lender has obtained a lender's policy, but the owner continues to make his mortgage payments each and every month until the mortgage is paid in full. The lender, therefore, has no loss, and the title policy will never have to pay. That is a key reason lender's title policies are less expensive.

Question. So what do owners need to do to be sure their equity is covered?

Response. To repair title problems for the owner and cover equity in the property, the owner would have had to purchase an owner's policy.

Myth 3—The Former Owner's Title Policy Benefits the New Owner

Truth. Each buyer needs to purchase a new policy.

Question. I am assuming the seller's four-year-old loan. Because the seller already has an owner's policy, my title should be clear, right?

Response. Title changes constantly, and because the owner's policy was written four years ago, there could be many changes in the interim that would affect your title. The owner could have added an addition to the house that caused mechanics' liens; had judgments filed against her or him; gone bankrupt; or been divorced. All of these items cause title problems for you, the buyer. Title needs to be checked every time a property is sold or mortgaged. To protect yourself, you need a new owner's policy.

Question. I bought an owner's policy when I purchased the house three years ago. But now I am refinancing with a new lender. Do I need to update my owner's policy and buy a new one?

Response. No, your owner's policy protects you for as long as you own the property. Under the terms of the policy, it will also protect you after you sell the property if you give a warranty deed and a title problem is discovered later, because warranty deeds warrant title into the future and you retain liability after the sale. However, in this case, there is no need to buy a new owner's policy. Nevertheless, remember the new lender needs a new lender's policy to assure a first lien position at closing, and to protect them against outstanding judgments, liens, or encumbrances that affect title and have occurred since the previous loan.

Myth 4—Title Insurance Is Just Like Other Types of Insurance

Truth. Title insurance is very different from other forms of insurance.

Most insurance covers future risks. Title insurance is different. Its primary function is to *uncover and repair current and past risks before the policy is issued.* Companies that provide life insurance, health insurance, fire insurance, car insurance, and so on, take on future risks according to carefully calculated actuarial and historical tables. They have strong histories that predict how long someone will live; the average cost of a doctor appointment; how often and in what neighborhoods fires will happen; or how often an 18-year-old boy will have a car accident. Unlike other insurances, no actuarial tables exist to determine such things for title insurers. Volume of errors made in the public offices or statistics on numbers of fraudulent real estate transactions affecting title do not exist. And, because real estate transactions are highly sensitive to interest rates, which have varied considerably in the last few years and affect the volume of documents recorded, title risks cannot be set by actuarial tables.

Title insurance covers current, past, and now some future risks. While title companies have traditionally taken on only *current* and *past* risks, the new 2008 product has been expanded to make it more attractive to homebuyers by covering a number of *future* risks. Under the terms of the new 2008 ALTA Homeowner's Policy, it covers several things occurring after the policy date.

For example, the policy states it will give coverage if, "because of an existing violation of a subdivision law or regulation affecting the land:

a. You are unable to obtain a building permit;
b. You are required to correct or remove the violation."

Risk elimination causes fewer claims. As opposed to other insurances, the title insurance industry is primarily one of **risk elimination** and not **risk assumption**. Title companies attempt to eliminate as many risks as possible by thoroughly scrutinizing matters that disclose possible interests in title. This includes searching the land records, tax records, court records, and municipal records, as well as studying documents for indications of fraud, forgery, and so on. It means asking questions, getting identification, and taking affidavits from buyers and sellers as to their knowledge of facts. Often a survey is ordered or an inspection is requested where someone physically looks at the property to determine location of improvements, what parties are in possession, and if there are signs of easements. An inspector may also look for recent repairs or improvements that might indicate existence of mechanics' liens—all to eliminate risk.

Myth 5—Title Insurers Pay Few Claims

Truth. Lenders and buyers have never been at greater risk for a title claim.

The risk climate has changed and claims are soaring. Since 2006, the title insurance industry, as the entire real estate industry, has seen significant change. This includes a dramatic increase in the number of claims that can be attributed to a number of rapidly changing factors:

- One major reason is the phenomenal real estate boom between 2000 and 2006. This increased flurry of activity and sheer volume resulted in numerous claims based on mistakes made both by title examiners and by closing attorneys and staff, particularly inexperienced new title agents.

- Less careful investigation of titles has taken place over the last few years. Title insurers perceived that lenders wanted an instant title search. So, for example, in order to meet the clients desire to close a home equity loan within 24 hours, new limited search products were developed and made available. Many of these products are being produced in China, the Philippines, India, and other foreign countries, using less expensive but less skilled personnel for the search of records and the examination of title, resulting in more claims. Quality of some title products has deteriorated. A quote from the National Association of Land Title Examiners and Abstractors (*www.NALTEA.org*) states:

  "There has been an absence of corrective action in recent title work. Many title agents and underwriters have cut corners to put out a cheapened product as fast as possible. They have been lax and slipshod in properly documenting payoffs of mortgages in particular. This improper title work is often a direct result of inadequate public records searches, resulting in a drastic increase in title claims. When the amount paid in claims—together with the cost of defending against claims—begins to outweigh the savings realized from cutting corners with inexperienced and untrained overseas staff, the result can only be higher title insurance premiums. The National Association of Land Title Examiners and Abstractors believes title insurers are now paying a price for poor quality that will ultimately result in higher prices for the consumer."

- Another worrisome area includes liability for closing problems, such as accepting noncollected funds at closing (e.g., a bounced check from the lender or buyer); accommodating their best client's promise that a lien "really has been removed" (with proof to follow); or a second mortgage or equity line being recorded *before* the insured mortgage. Here is a typical example. A title company conducted a title search on a property in New York revealing Marilyn and Erving Bohaty, husband and wife, in title. The purchase agreement was signed only by Marilyn, who told the title company of her divorce. On the day of closing, a faded copy of the divorce decree was faxed to the closer showing Marilyn in title, free and clear of Erving's interest. The closer obtained permission to close without a deed from Erving. She collected money for obtaining a certified copy of the divorce decree and for recording it in the county office. Several weeks later, the title company recieved the certified copy, only to learn the faxed copy was doctored. Erving was given a $60,000 lien on the property, due on sale. Erv, of course, found out about the sale and sued. The title company had to pay the claim to clear the title.

- Title underwriters have also been forced by demands from the market to begin insuring the closing process, not only of their own branch offices but also of their agents. This has become a dangerous and expensive proposition in today's market. Closing was not originally intended to be part of the insuring of titles, and risks pertaining to closing problems were not accrued for. In some states (New York, for example) the state insurance commissioner has determined that closing is a separate risk that may not be underwritten by a title insurer. In any case, additional liability for additional risk means the cost of doing business will go up and closing costs will continue to rise.

- Other major reasons deal with illegal matters such as identity theft, fraud, and forgery that are becoming rampant in our society. Everyone is aware that identity theft has become a major problem in the United States. This includes the title industry. For example, there are cases where lessees, in possession of a property, put themselves in title by recording a fraudulent deed from the owners to themselves. Having checked the public record, the title company then helped the fraudulent owner put a (fraudulent) mortgage of record. After all, an apparently good deed was of record, the party was in possession, and all appeared well. The real owner continued to receive payments on the lease, paid for by the mortgage the lessee had taken on the owner's property. Such creativity!

- Because of the large dollar amounts handled in real estate sales, it is a prime target for these and other scams. The National Association of Insurance Commissioners Report to U.S. House of Representatives of April 26, 2006 (*www.naic.org/documents/govt_rel_issues_title_testimony_0604_toll.pdf*), stated that "...title insurance's uniqueness provides fertile ground for certain questionable activities." Google shows more than 20 million entries for identity theft alone. In the past, title insurers never conceived of bearing these types of risks as title insurance risks, but they are now being forced toward casualty insurance in these areas. Here is another case in point. "California Battles Growing Wave of Real Estate Fraud" is the title to an article from a California newspaper about a professional fraudster who leased a house through a real estate agent. The fraudster moved in and checked the public record to find out who was in title. The fraudster, pretending to be the owner, then called another unsuspecting real estate agent and told him that he had been offered an excellent job opportunity, out of town, if he could start the position in just three weeks. So he needed a quick sale. The agent listed the property at a price significantly under market value in order to get that quick sale. At the amazingly low price, the house sold immediately and proceeded toward closing. The title company checked the record, had a survey, and investigated parties and possession (the fraudster was in possession using the real owner's name). At closing, the fraudulent "owner" brought in forged identity papers and collected the sales price on the house. Only months later, when the real owners returned to town, did they find that their furniture was gone and the new "owners" had moved in. Hopefully, the unsuspecting buyers bought an owner's policy!

Also, claim dollars and losses have increased due to the creativity and success of lawsuits against title insurance companies. Plaintiffs have been successful under theories of recovery that were never contemplated under the terms of the original title insurance policy, and juries tend to favor a homeowner's claim over the terms and conditions set forth in the policy of a large title insurance company. Closings, mortgages, and legal documents are becoming much more complex, which adds fuel to an already complicated system and more fodder for lawsuits. Ethical standards of a number of title insurers, agents, and approved attorneys have caused losses to title companies. Defalcation claims in which the agent or approved attorney embezzles funds held in escrow have substantially increased over the past few years. These kinds of claims are particularly destructive since there are generally few assets left against which recovery can be made once the dust has settled.

> Discussion: Take three or four minutes to identify some title problems encountered in transactions of which you are aware. How and when were these problems resolved?

Myth 6—Title Insurance Is Expensive

Truth. In the scope of costs for buying and selling a house, title insurance is a bargain. For a small one-time fee, the price of the home is secured for a lifetime. Balance the cost of title insurance with the following:

- *One-time premium.* Life, health, property, and casualty insurance charge premiums every year for a one-year period of coverage. Title companies charge premiums once only. They do not have the opportunity to adjust for potential losses as times change. Title insurance for a lender lasts until the mortgage is paid off, sometimes 50 years. And, while an owner's policy generally continues in force until the property is sold, it will cover the sellers even after closing when they give a deed warranting good title if title problems later appear. An owner's policy can continue indefinitely as when written to a corporation or trust. A.M. Best in the October, 2003, *Special Report* states, "By the nature of the business, most title losses are reported in paid within the first five to seven years after policy issuance. However, the tale [*period for which claims occur*] for title policies is at least 20 years." (A.M. Best Company, Inc. Special Report dated October 20, 2003. Report written by Gary A. Davis, analyst, A.M. Best, and Richard McCarthy, Director of Research, ALTA.)

  In the above-cited NAIC report, it states: "Compared to both the overall cost of the home buying process and other insurance lines, title insurance is inexpensive…" "The average yearly cost of health insurance is about $2,400 a year or $96,000 over one's lifetime. The average yearly cost of auto insurance is about $1,000 or roughly $40,000 over one's lifetime." The report cites an example: "In Colorado, the cost of title insurance for a $300,000 home is about $1,000. Given that the average person buys six homes in a lifetime, an average consumer may pay $6,000 for title insurance over the course of their lifetime (taking refinances out of the equation for simplicity) and have only six contacts with a title insurer. On the other hand, consumers have many contacts with auto and health insurers and pay more for these products over their lifetime."

- *High cost of doing business.* Because title insurance requires such detailed work to thoroughly examine title and reduce risks, its loss expense has been less than other insurers, but its cost of doing business is significantly higher than other insurance lines. Out-of-pocket operating expenses, primarily due to obtaining public records and professional staffing costs to determine insurability, are a title company's largest expense.

- *Expenses incurred before payment.* Unlike property and casualty insurers, title companies collect premiums after their expenses have been incurred. And, if for any reason a transaction does not close, title companies will often receive no compensation for their work or their out-of-pocket expenses—just like a real estate agent.

However, title premiums are currently in flux. Although government regulators acknowledge that the cost is a reasonable expense in the big picture, they have required reductions in premium costs in many states after studying the claims history of the industry. The NAIC report to the U.S. House of Representatives of 2006 (*www.naic.org/documents/govt_rel_issues_title_testimony_0604_toll.pdf*) states: "One of the unusual characteristics of title insurance is that so few claims are paid. Over

10 years, all 86 title insurers [*studied*] across the country paid slightly more than 5 cents out in claims for every dollar of premium consumers paid.

"Compare this to other lines of insurance:

- Homeowners: 75 cents for every dollar
- Auto: 60 cents for every dollar
- Health maintenance organizations: 86 cents for every dollar"

"The title agency normally retains 85 to 90 percent of the premium, and the remaining 10 to 15 percent goes to the insurer. Title insurance is a flat, one-time fee paid along with a host of other fees, as part of a large, complex transaction."

Myth 7—Very Few Files Have Title Problems

Truth. The American Land Title Association (ALTA) is a national trade association of the abstract and title insurance industries. ALTA members search, review, and insure land titles to protect homebuyers and mortgage lenders who invest in real estate. Members of the association are in business in most counties across the nation, ranging from small, one-county operations, to large national title insurers. Associate members of ALTA include attorneys, builders, developers, lenders, real estate brokers, surveyors, consultants, educators, and related national trade associations.

An ALTA study in 2004 showed that *one in four* files have title defects! (ALTA press release September 27, 2004, *www.alta.org/press/release.cfm?newsID=2171*).

Title insurance losses have never been higher, meaning that more and more files have title problems, and more and more money is being paid in claims. Title companies admit that many more title problems come to light when the real-estate market is weak. Title problems frequently turn up during a foreclosure, and as foreclosures rise, claims often follow. Most title insurance policies are held by lenders that file claims during the foreclosure process as problems appear. The foreclosure market is strong. It gets worse. Reports for 2007 to date on the financial aspects for the title industry have been, at best, dismal. Virtually all title underwriters showing significant losses quarter after quarter on their financial statements since 2006. It is common for claims in a single quarter to be up 50 percent or more from the same quarter of the previous year. Steep drops in earnings, deep staff cuts and seriously declining stock prices complete the picture. Another issue for underwriters is that under economic stress title agents often do not pass along premium payments promptly; however, the insurer still must honor any policies. Real estate has always been somewhat volatile and cyclical. So, the question is not will the industry come back; the question is when.

The bottom line: The increasingly complex nature of the business, along with the heavy real estate volume from 2000 to 2006, put a tremendous strain on all portions of the industry—mortgage bankers and banks, real estate agents, builders, appraisers, county recorders, and others were inundated with more work than they had ever experienced. This led to the creation of many new and inexperienced title agencies, particularly affiliated business associations jumping on to what was perceived as a lucrative new side venture to their already existing real estate, home building, or lending businesses. And title insurers created new and innovative ways of doing business using shortcuts, many of which were later shown to be poor choices that led to increasing errors and significant title claims. All in all, showing a title policy to be not only a good investment but also a critical investment for both the lender and the buyer!

Myth 8—Title Companies Rarely Pay

Truth. Because title companies formerly spent so much money researching and helping to clear potential problems before closing, their losses were historically *low*. Increases over the years have been quite moderate. But claims and losses are now historically *high*.

An ALTA press release stated that about one in four titles searched identify title problems that need resolution prior to closing (ALTA press release of September 27, 2004). Obviously, the dollars paid out in claims are *not* the result of the one in four problems that were identified and thus resolved, but rather the more insidious, unidentified problems.

Under the terms of the policy, title insurers pay to defend *all* claims, regardless of whether the claim is legitimate. Defending claims is a significant dollar expense. Costs of legal defense have skyrocketed. Attorney fees, court fees, and professional witness fees are significant expenses to a title company regardless of the outcome of a case. Also, title policies do not have a dollar limit on the insurers' duty to defend, and legal expenses paid by the insurers do not reduce the policy amount. However, common sense says insurers will try to keep their losses at a minimum. This means that the insurers may elect to pay the face amount of the policy should they deem the claim a total loss, or deem it more expensive to defend the case than to pay the claim.

One title underwriter is currently facing a single title claim payment of $50 million. While the underwriter was prudent enough to reinsure, the thought of a single $50 million loss is frightening.

■ Summary

The title industry is an important but often misunderstood business. In truth, it does not guarantee good title, but provides a monetary indemnity against loss. It is unlike other forms of insurance in that it primarily covers current and past events but has been stretched now to cover some future events. Insurers lessen their risk by searching many public records, doing an examination of title, and asking questions to solve and ward off numerous title problems prior to closing, before issuing the policy. It is inexpensive, relative to other forms of insurance, as it requires only a fairly small one-time payment compared to the value of the property; and it covers a host of title problems, such as problems with recorded documents, fraud, forgery, and identity theft, as well as some items that may occur in the future. Like the real estate industry, the title industry struggles with a fluctuating market.

Title insurance is not generally a topic that real estate agents and brokers study or spend time on. There is a tendency to "leave it to the closer" to review the title work, rather than trying to understand what the title work says. By understanding the title work, and knowing the truths about title insurance, agents can help their clients make an informed decision about buying an owner's policy of title insurance. Also, with the risk involved in handling hundreds of thousands of dollars on each transaction, an agent can protect buyers' and sellers' money by getting a closing protection letter from the title underwriter for his or her clients.

case study

Your client is purchasing what may be a considered a "high-risk" title. The sellers, George and Karen Rellings, inherited the property from a deceased uncle, and they are only willing to give a quitclaim deed on the property. They have had to do about $30,000 in repairs to bring the property up to code for the sale, and mechanics' liens have been filed. The uncle has a common name, and there are numerous judgments against that name. The Rellings have no idea if the judgments were against the uncle or not, nor do they claim to know anything about the title.

The closing is scheduled to occur with a title agency that has just opened its doors. In fact, you are its first closing—congratulations. The owner of the title agency is a cousin of the loan officer.

Your buyer does not know if she should buy an owner's title policy on the $235,000 home. She thinks it is quite expensive. What can you tell her to help her decide and what should she request of the title company?

Review Questions

1. ALTA studies show that what percentage of files have title defects?
   a. 2
   b. 5
   c. 10
   d. 25

2. Title insurance _____ that a person can retain title and possession of property under any circumstances.
   a. defends the title so
   b. affirms
   c. provides an insurance policy stating
   d. cannot guarantee

3. Title insurers
   a. guarantee title will not be challenged.
   b. assume the likelihood of a claim is minimal.
   c. will insure over any problem, if so requested.
   d. assume the monetary risk of title problems from the insured.

4. The best title examination cannot detect or identify
   a. fraud.
   b. a forged signature on a document.
   c. an unrecorded document.
   d. All of the above

5. What estimated percentage of U.S. homeowners don't have an owner's title policy?
   a. 5
   b. 20
   c. 40
   d. 60

6. The title insurance policy that most likely decreases in value over time is a(n)
   a. owner's policy.
   b. leasehold policy.
   c. mortgage policy.
   d. None of the above

7. Which of the following is *NOT* assignable?
   a. An owner's policy
   b. A leasehold policy
   c. A mortgage policy
   d. An easement estate policy

8. An owner's title policy provides a contractual duty to defend
   a. all closing claims.
   b. lender's and owner's title problems.
   c. lien and encroachments problems only.
   d. all claims covered under the policy.

9. Which statement is *TRUE* about title premiums?
   a. They are decreasing because less investigation is done on property than previously.
   b. They are a reasonable buy in a claims filled environment.
   c. They have remained stable, due to the large volume of business in recent years.
   d. They are increasing throughout the country.

10. Title underwriters and agents
    a. are stable, due to strong long-term profitability.
    b. are stronger than ever due to excellent financial controls.
    c. remain consistently solid, due to sound underwriting and claims management.
    d. suffer from the volatility of a fluctuating market.

chapter four

How to Read Title Work Like a Title Professional

learning objectives

After completing this chapter, you will be able to

- define the most common title encumbrances and explain, in plain English, what they mean to a customer (common title issues that are generally expected and acceptable have a "thumbs up" icon next to them);
- distinguish what's acceptable on title work from what's not acceptable;
- know how to review title work to assure it meets a customer's needs; and

- recognize red flag areas that will likely delay closing unless given special attention (potential pitfalls for closing that need special attention have a "thumbs down" icon next to them; review them carefully).

■ Key Terms

assessment	effective date	pending assessments
blanket easement	encroachment	purchase-money
boilerplate	escrow	mortgage
cloud on title	forfeiture clause	right of first refusal
commitment to insure	general liens	Schedule A
covenants, conditions,	impact fee	Schedule B
and restrictions	levied assessments	specific liens
(CC&Rs)	notice of lis pendens	standard exceptions
easement	novation	title binder

What Is the Title Commitment?

The *title commitment*, also known as the **commitment to insure,** or **title binder**, is *the* document that reflects all of the title research done on property through a particular date called the *effective date*. The **effective date** is a snapshot in time, telling what title looked like at a particular moment. The purpose of the title commitment is to

- inform all parties of any encumbrances affecting the property, and
- commit to insure property, subject to certain stated requirements.

The title commitment outlines the title procedure for purchasers and lenders to close the transaction. It allows the parties to determine what "rights" are acceptable to them and what must be resolved to satisfy their needs.

Parts of the Title Commitment

The title commitment is generally divided into sections: "cover sheet" or "jacket," Schedule A, and Schedule B. Schedule B is sometimes divided into Schedule B-1 and Schedule B-2.

By understanding the layout of the commitment (the jacket and schedules), interested parties can get a quick handle on the information.

Cover Sheet or Jacket

The cover sheet has the same standard language for all commitments and provides generic information. It explains the following:

- The commitment is good only for a certain amount of time (generally six months), at which time it must be endorsed (modified) to provide current information, or it will terminate.
- The terms of the policy (covered in Chapter 5, Understanding Title Policies).
- Liability is limited to the amount stated in the commitment and the parties listed as proposed insureds.
- The title company reserves the right to amend the commitment to reflect any changes in, or new, information.
- How to contact the title company.

Schedule A

Precise information about the specific transaction used for closing and to create legal documents is listed on **Schedule A.** It shows the following:

- The "effective date" (date through which the public record has been searched, not the current date)
- Names of lender and/or buyer to be insured (John Q. Doe, single)
- Type of policy to be issued (homeowners' policy and/or loan policy)
- Sale price when an owner's policy is being issued ($259,000)
- Loan amount when a lender's policy is being issued ($215,000)
- The estate being insured (fee simple, vendee's interest, leasehold estate, etc.)
- Exactly how sellers currently hold title (Peter D. Sellers and Mary Jo Sellers, husband and wife, as joint tenants)

- Precise legal description for the property (frequently the address and tax parcel number are shown for reference)

Schedule B

All title issues pertaining to the property being insured are listed on **Schedule B.** This is the meat of the title and the key to closing the transaction. Schedule B states, "The policy will be issued subject to the following exceptions, unless they are disposed of to the satisfaction of the title company." This is where the agent, closer, buyers, and sellers need to concentrate their efforts and review and understand each item—item by item.

Note that some companies will list all issues under one Schedule B, while others will divide them up into two schedules: Schedule B-1, often being those items that will remain on the policy, and Schedule B-2, being those items the title company anticipates to be removed at the time of closing. Here we will discuss Schedule B as a single schedule.

Typically the "boilerplate" language comes first. **Boilerplate** is the standard or preprinted language in a document that is the same from transaction to transaction. For example, with a FNMA mortgage the language is standard for all loans, except for the fill-in blanks. The boilerplate almost always starts with four **standard exceptions** pertaining to (1) parties in possession, (2) easements not shown by the public record, (3) questions of survey, and (4) unrecorded mechanics' liens. Other more localized standard exceptions may appear here as well. In some parts of the country, these items may be removed with receipt of appropriate inspection, plat, survey, or other remedies. Generally, these first standard exception items are consistent from transaction to transaction, and you should find no surprises here.

Below the boilerplate language are all of the "exceptions" to coverage that apply specifically to the property described in the commitment. Schedule B may also continue with some fairly obvious instructions to the closer, such as "We require:

- "payment to the grantors for the purchase of the property;
- "proper instruments (deeds) to be executed and recorded, specifically a deed from seller John C. Doe, and spouse, if any, to Mary Lee Smith, a single person, the buyer and/or a mortgage to ABC Lender, a Massachusetts Corporation;
- "payment of all outstanding taxes and assessments; and
- "signing an affidavit as to nonrecord title matters." As previously discussed, the affidavits ask the buyers and sellers, under oath, if there are any unpaid judgments against them, if they have furnished any material or labor to the premises for which payment has not been made, if any proceedings have been filed in bankruptcy court, if there are any changes in marital status, and so on.

■ Reading Title Work—Title Exceptions Found on Nearly All Property

Real Estate Taxes

Taxation is a government right to raise revenue by charging fees against real estate. Title companies search public county and/or city offices to locate current and delinquent taxes.

Status. Taxes are ACCEPTABLE as an exception to title; taxation is always a government right. A few properties such as government-owned and some owned by religious and nonprofit organizations are exempt. Taxes are generally shown as the first item on title work.

Current tax information, such as the tax amount, due date, and a tax parcel number, are included. Other information, such as whether the property is homestead or not homestead (for tax purposes), and if there are any assessment installments due within the tax payment, may also be shown. (Tax homestead is a property tax classification and is *not* to be confused with legal homestead, which is a court judgment exempting a home from most general debts, such as judgments.) This information provides the closer with facts and figures so that he or she can fill in correct numbers on the closing statement and comply with the requirements of the purchase agreement or sales contract as to proration of taxes.

Delinquent tax information, including the delinquent tax amount and penalties due, is also shown for collection at closing according to the terms of the purchase agreement or sales contract.

Assessments

An **assessment** is a charge, generally for the improvement of the property, such as street improvements or sewer or water system upgrades, but it may also cover ongoing expenses such as street lighting or garbage collection. Title companies must search counties and/or cities to locate assessments.

Status. They are ACCEPTABLE as an exception to title; assessments are always a government right. Payment or assumption of the assessments is settled at closing according to the terms of the purchase agreement or sales contract.

There are two primary forms of assessments. Levied assessments mean improvements are complete and can be paid. Levied assessments will be shown in detail. What the assessment is for, the outstanding balance, and the length of time over which the assessment may be paid will all be shown. A portion of the levied assessment is added to the tax statement yearly until paid.

Pending assessments are proposed assessments that are not yet complete, whose exact cost is unknown, and that cannot yet be paid. Depending on how the purchase agreement is written, an estimated amount (usually one and one-half to two times the estimate) will be held or **escrowed** from the seller or buyer for future payment.

Easements

An **easement** is an authorized use of land for a specific purpose. Title companies locate easements by checking recorded documents against the legal description of the property, examining recorded plats and maps, and obtaining a survey or inspection that would show physical evidence of an easement, such as a telephone pole or fire hydrant. A typical example on title work might read: "An easement over the north ten feet of property for purposes of utilities and drainage." This is a legal right that can only be used for utility and drainage purposes and only over the north ten feet, not for a party, general access, or other reason.

Status. Easements are generally ACCEPTABLE on title work; see exceptions below.

Note that easements can be positive by adding to the value of property, or negative by taking away some use of the property. Generally, they add to the value by providing gas, electrical, cable, and other services to the property. In some cases, an easement (for access, for example), is critical to a transaction and must be insured. In other cases, the sales price is heavily reliant on an easement. For example, Kevin is purchasing a lot across the street from a lake together with an easement for lake access. The lake access makes the lot worth $200,000 more and also should be insured along with the lot.

Buyers should specifically be made aware when a commitment says something like the following:

> "Easement over the west 20 feet of subject property for the purpose of the laying, maintaining, and repairing of utility lines."

The easement above limits the owners' use of the west 20 feet of their property, and they should not plant, dig, or in any way block that west 20 feet. Owners should be made aware of the location of all easements on their property.

Utility and drainage easements. These are by far the most common easements found on properties. Generally, there is nothing to do about a positive utility and/or drainage easement.

Comment. From a practical standpoint, agents want to tell their customers where the easement is, how big it is, and what it is used for. Customers should be made aware of any easements and the fact that they should not plant or obstruct the easement as digging could be dangerous, and any improvements made on the easements may have to be removed.

Encroachment problem. An *encroachment* is an illegal intrusion onto another person's right and is NOT ACCEPTABLE. If an encroachment exists, title work will disclose the problem, because the title company will have received a survey, inspection or some type of plat drawing that would disclose the encroachment.

For example, say the title work discloses the seller has built a garage that encroaches onto the neighbor's property by about two feet. Your buyer still wants the property but is concerned about the encroachment. You could discuss the possibility of obtaining an owner's policy with an endorsement to "insure over" (or guaranty against forced removal of the structure) for the problem, or look at purchasing an easement from the neighbor for the right to maintain the garage as currently located. The title company can help with these decisions.

Blanket easement. A *blanket easement* is an undefined easement, one that has been recorded over a large parcel of land with no location or limits as to its width. One key issue with a blanket easement is that it can be expanded until released. This means that if, for example, the phone company has a blanket easement over a large parcel of land, and you can see the location of power lines that do not run near your property, the phone company can continue to put up lines, as they deem necessary until the easement is released.

Status. This MAY OR MAY NOT BE ACCEPTABLE; a blanket easement is handled differently in different parts of the country. In some locations it is considered customary and acceptable, in other areas it is considered a problem. Check with your title company for assistance.

Comment. Blanket easements are sometimes considered problematic. Ideally, a blanket easement should be defined as to actual location and width, and the balance of the land released.

Common driveway easements. These occur when two or more parties use the same physical property for access, and they are typical in most parts of the country. The easement may be on one parcel or may be split across two or more parcels.

Status. They are generally ACCEPTABLE on title work.

Comment. In some cases, access over someone else's property is the *only* access. A written easement agreement will be required, and title to the easement will have to be examined and insured. All title policies guarantee legal access. Note that this does *not* include physical access and the owner may need to build a road to drive onto the land; it just includes the legal right of ingress and egress.

Comment. For your customer's sake, inquire about the common driveway to find out the course of action as to when and how the road is repaired, and how costs of maintenance are incurred.

Wetlands or environmental easements. These are easements that must be maintained in their natural state pursuant to environmental protection acts.

Status. ACCEPTABLE on title work, but owners must be aware they cannot remove existing vegetation or wetlands, nor can they improve that portion of the property covered in the wetlands or environmental easement. Environmental easements are becoming much more commonplace.

Mortgages/deeds of trust. These are legal documents that pledge a piece of property as security for a debt.

Status. Generally ACCEPTABLE on title work; mortgages are either assumed (not all loans are assumable) or paid at closing. If the loan is being assumed, you may want to consider having your seller released from liability under the terms of the mortgage and mortgage note. While this generally requires the buyer to qualify for the new mortgage, and there is often a fee for this service, it is a safety precaution for the sellers who are *still liable for the mortgage and note if they are not released*. The legal term for replacing the liability of the sellers with the buyers is **novation**.

Problem. Often, people are not aware that they have more than one mortgage on their property. Examples follow:

- Sam and Sally Tanaka know they have a $10,000 "equity line" at their bank. They acquired it to pay off some high-interest-rate credit cards, but they did not realize that what their bank termed an "equity line" is actually a second mortgage on their property that has to be paid at closing.
- John and Mary Ramon were advised by their financial consultant to take out a "line of credit" to purchase a new vehicle because the interest payable on the loan would be tax deductible, saving them money. They were unaware

when they signed the papers that their home secures the $32,000 line of credit.
- Thomas and Suzanne Johnson remembered paying off their home equity line of credit, but they did not close the account. When they overdrew their checking account to pay college tuition, the $4,000 balance went back onto their home under the terms of the line of credit.

These transactions mean the credit cards are paid down, and the car is paid, the child is still in college, but these sellers will be netting out much less—$10,000, $32,000, and $4,000 respectively—for the purchase of new homes than they expected!

Before closing, be sure to discuss with your sellers *all* the mortgages shown on the title work.

Comment. The single most common title problem found today is a mortgage that has been paid in full, but whose "paperwork" is missing or incorrect. Because lenders sell "mortgage servicing" without assigning the loan, change their name, merge with other companies, and frequently assign their mortgages to other companies, the paperwork can be a mess!

Unreleased mortgages/deeds of trust are NOT ACCEPTABLE. It is often necessary to obtain old mortgage information, such as loan numbers or servicing agents, in order to resolve the problem.

A fairly new "movement" within the country is for title companies to create and file a "satisfaction of mortgages by title company" at the time the title company pays off the mortgage debt. This type of release requires state legislation to be effective, but it does resolve a lot of satisfaction of mortgage issues.

Covenants, Conditions, and Restrictions

> Any time you see CC&Rs, you want your buyers to review the entire document. They need to know what they can and cannot do to and on the property!

Covenants, conditions, and restrictions (CC&Rs) are legally enforceable limitations on the use of land. Title companies search the public record looking for both restrictions contained within recorded deeds, or separate documents that lay out restrictions for an entire subdivision. Contained within any of these documents can be hidden costs pertaining to future expenses for maintenance or even beautification.

Status. Generally CC&Rs are ACCEPTABLE on title work. They typically come in two forms. They are either

1. *deed restrictions*, that is, they were placed inside a single deed upon the sale of the property in order to limit use of a specific property, or
2. *covenants, conditions, and restrictions*, that is, a separate, recorded document covering many parcels and typically recorded against an entire subdivision. Restrictions affect both current and future use of the property and are appurtenant, or "run with the land."

Agents need to be familiar with CC&Rs and how they will impact the buyer's use of the property.

Comment. Many older restrictions are outlawed by federal law. Even though recorded against the land, if CC&Rs restrict property based on race, color, religion, creed, national origin, sex, sexual orientation, marital or familial status, and so on, they are unenforceable and are still ACCEPTABLE.

Title companies, when asked, will give endorsements to insure against their enforceability, if a customer deems it necessary. However, in most cases, people do not see this as a problem because they know the restrictions are not enforceable. Title companies will not pay to have the documents "expunged" (i.e., legally removed from the public record), however, as it is deemed an unnecessary expense, although some restrictions may be offensive to some people.

Problem. Some restrictions, most commonly found in a deed restriction, contain a **forfeiture clause,** a reversionary statement that could cause loss of the property. Forfeiture clauses are NOT ACCEPTABLE on title work; they are "deadly." While many older forfeiture clauses are unenforceable, many still exist that are enforceable.

Example: A deed restrictions states, "Subject to the restriction that this property will be used and maintained as a recreational park for the benefit of the public forever, to be known as the 'Jeanine Johnson Memorial Park.' In the event it is not so used, it will revert to the Grantor, her heirs, and/or assigns."

A mortgage company will not lend funds on a property with a forfeiture restriction because it is not salable in the secondary market. Can this property be sold? Yes, it can, subject to the restriction. However, if the restriction is violated, the property will revert to its previous owner, her heirs, and/or assigns.

Look for an important statement on title work insuring that any restrictions "do not contain a forfeiture provision." All listed restrictions should have this clause printed on the title commitment.

Comment. Housing and redevelopment authorities (HRAs), historical societies, and government agencies often restrict their property sales.

Covenants, conditions, and restrictions MAY OR MAY NOT BE ACCEPTABLE, depending on your local market. Consider the following examples:

- The Historical Society might require that a home be maintained or restored to its original condition, according to certain defined standards such as "this property will be maintained in the original condition the Victorian home was built (with a list of the authentic Victorian standards attached)." Even if there is no forfeiture provision attached, the buyers will be subject to legal action if they do not maintain the residence in its original condition according to the defined terms.
- Housing and redevelopment authorities often provide low-interest-rate loans to improve neighborhoods. The loan might require a house be brought up to a certain code and that the buyers agree to live in it for a certain length of time before it can be sold. Or there may be a dollar penalty payable to the HRA if the property is resold before a certain date. Again, these documents may even include a forfeiture provision to the authority. So read the title work carefully. Sometimes, a release can be obtained to clear the objection.

Comment. Depending on the circumstances, the owners should obtain a release or be prepared to comply with the restriction. If they do not comply, they risk legal recourse and possible loss of the property.

Comment. Common CC&Rs in residential areas frequently exist. CC&Rs are generally ACCEPTABLE. Most residential communities have covenants, conditions, and restrictions that were designed to maintain continuity within an area and make the neighborhood feel more cohesive. They often include required building sizes, number of pets allowed, and can cover architectural controls as to color, plantings, etc.

Comment. When purchasers buy into a neighborhood with CC&Rs, they should be fully aware of what those restrictions are and be aware that they are enforceable. After all, the buyers must live with those conditions!

> Discussion: What are some common covenants, conditions, and restrictions on single-family and condominium units in your market?

Common Interest Communities and Restrictions

CC&Rs exist on common interest communities (CICs), also known as planned unit developments (PUDs), such as town houses, condominiums, cooperatives, and time-shares often in the form of a "Declaration." Title companies have to go to extraordinary lengths to obtain information on each subdivision's restrictions, particularly because they obtain the right to assess homeowners within the subdivision for common area expenses and violations of homeowner rules.

CC&Rs on common interest communities are both ACCEPTABLE and NECESSARY. Because the owners share common walls and common areas such as parking, tot lots, and swimming pools, the legal consequences of who owns what and how to rebuild if there is a natural disaster or fire must be stated. Other items must also be addressed, such as how to pay for the shared expenses and how to respectfully use common areas must also be set forth.

Comment. When buyers move into a CIC, such as a town house, condominium, cooperative, time-share, or planned unit development, they are choosing a *lifestyle*. They must acknowledge and learn to deal with rules that they share in common with the neighbors. That usually means they do not get to choose

- the color of the building;
- how often snow is plowed or the lawn watered;
- how the grounds are maintained; or
- how they use the space outside the area they own (e.g., hanging wet clothes on their balcony).

The title company will tell you there are restrictions, but it may just refer you to a document number for details. Obtain the document and *read the document!* You and the buyers need to know what the restrictions are in order to know how they impact you. For example, can you answer the following questions?

- Do the restrictions allow your veterinarian client to *keep four pets* on the premises?
- Can your electrical contractor client *routinely park his trailer and/or truck in the common area* at the town house?
- Can your vegetarian buyer plant tomatoes and onions in the common area back yard?

Restrictions Impact Buyers

If the buyers do not like the restrictions and covenants, they are buying the wrong property. Help them find the *right* property. After all, if your client has a problem, you have a problem.

Comment. Shared community restrictions most often contain a requirement to pay association dues. This is ACCEPTABLE and even required on title work. In shared communities, this is standard.

Comment. A separate reference to the obligation to pay dues generally will be listed on the title commitment. Unpaid dues will be collected from the seller at time of closing. Unpaid dues are a lien on the land and "run with the land." Unpaid dues, even by previous owners, could result in the current owner having to pay them or risk losing the property. Buyers need to know such things as the following:

- How much the dues are
- How often the dues are paid
- What the dues cover: water, electric, cable TV, ongoing maintenance, sewer, water, reserves, etc.
- How and when dues can be raised
- If separate, additional special assessments can be charged per the restrictions and/or bylaws of the association as needs occur
- How much money is in the reserve account to cover major expenses such as roofing, roadways, etc. While some states *require* an association to hold adequate reserves for major expenses, other states allow an association to simply send out a notice of a special assessment to pay for needed repairs. The assessment could be thousands of dollars that the then current owner might have to pay.

Comment. CIC restrictions often contain a legal clause called a **right of first refusal**. While normally a formality, a right of first refusal gives the association the legal option to purchase a unit at fair market value; and that right needs to be extinguished. This is NOT ACCEPTABLE. The title company will request a letter from the homeowners' association, stating they do not wish to exercise the right of first refusal. The right of first refusal acts as a legal option to purchase.

Understanding and Removing Exceptions

In order to resolve problems, real estate professionals need to understand the title language. And, in order to understand title, we need to classify various title issues.

Encumbrances

The term *encumbrance* means any charge, claim, or liability against the title. It includes easements, restrictions, taxes, mechanics' liens, and many others. A *lien* is tied to a specific dollar amount. Therefore, you may not be able to remove an encumbrance, but you can always remove a lien, presuming there is enough money to do so. Typical liens include state and federal tax liens, attorneys' liens, mortgage liens, and judgment liens.

Specific liens. Liens are classified as either *specific* or *general*, *voluntary* or *involuntary*. **Specific liens** are liens secured by and recorded against specific prop-

Figure 4.1 | General versus Specific Liens

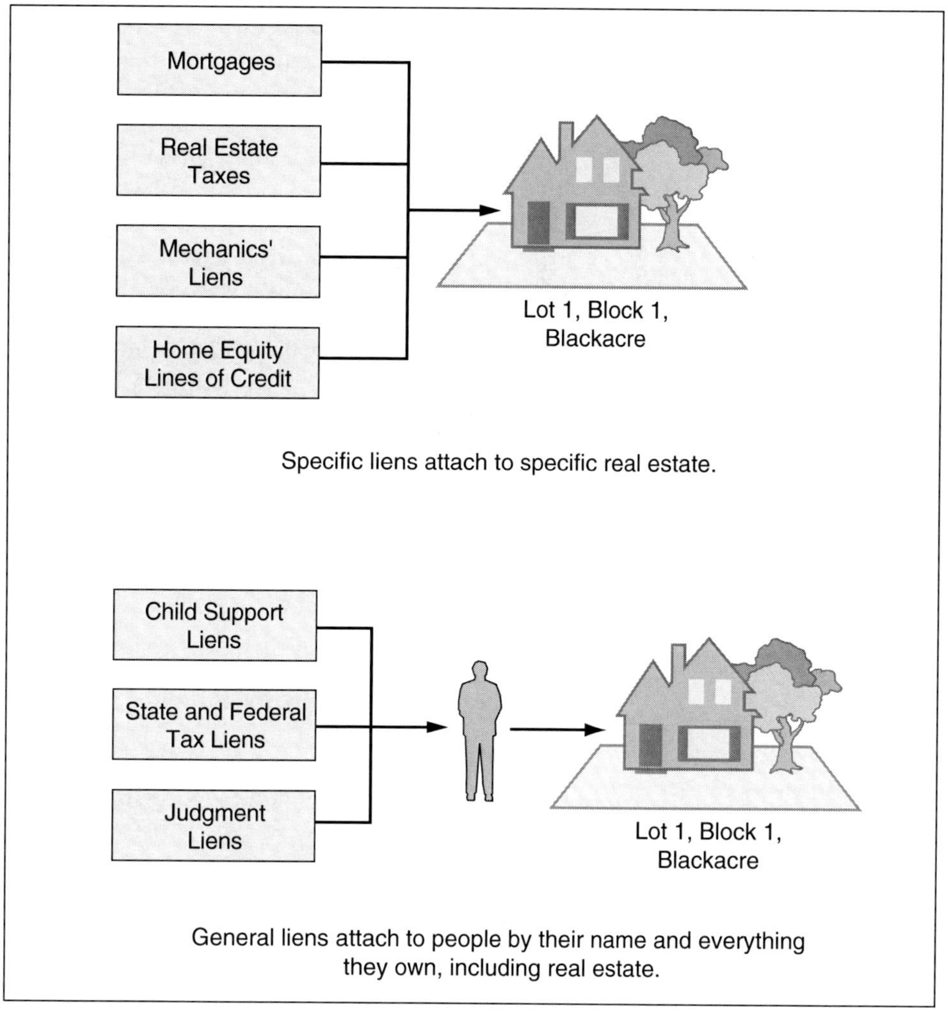

```
    Mortgages  ┐
               │
  Real Estate  │
     Taxes     ├──►  [House]
               │    Lot 1, Block 1,
  Mechanics'   │      Blackacre
    Liens      │
               │
  Home Equity  │
 Lines of Credit┘
```
Specific liens attach to specific real estate.

```
 Child Support ┐
    Liens      │
               │
 State and Federal├──► [Person] ──► [House]
   Tax Liens   │              Lot 1, Block 1,
               │                Blackacre
   Judgment    │
    Liens      ┘
```
General liens attach to people by their name and everything they own, including real estate.

erty and apply only to that specific real estate. Examples of this are mortgages, real estate taxes, and mechanics' liens. For example, a mortgage against Lot one, Block one, Blackacre stays with the land. If the owners, John and Jackie Smith, quit making payments on the mortgage, the bank will foreclose it and take title to the property. Assuming in the foreclosure that the bank was made whole, because the lien is a specific lien, it would disappear and would not attach to John and Jackie personally.

General liens. General liens, on the other hand, are filed against a person by his or her name, and attach to *all* of a person's property, both real and personal. (See Figure 4.1.) Examples of general liens include state tax liens, federal tax liens, and judgments, all of which are filed simply against a person's name. (But they are filed in many offices that vary by state, such as district courts, county courts, circuit court, county recorders' offices, federal courts, and many, many others.)

General liens affect only the property located where the lien is filed. In most cases this is the office of the county recorder, also known as the register of deeds, or wherever the land records are filed (sometimes city or parish). Sometimes land records are retained by the city (as in Connecticut and parts of the original 13 colonies) or in parishes (as in Louisiana), but in most states, land records are found in the office of the county recorder, register of deeds, or clerk of county court. For example, a general lien, such as a judgment filed in Lake County, CO, only affects property located in Lake County, CO. In order to affect property in Eagle County, CO, the judgment must again be filed in Eagle County.

If a judgment debtor sells his or her property, the lien should be paid at closing. If it is not paid, it remains a lien on the property he or she has just sold along with any other real and personal property owned by the judgment debtor. (Some exceptions, discussed later, apply with legally homesteaded property, which is not necessarily the same as tax homesteaded property.)

For example, John Shelby has a $2,400 judgment filed against him in Cass County. He is selling his Cass County home to his friend, Joe Smith. Because they are friends, they are not using a real estate agent, and there is no title search. Joe thinks he is getting a good deal on the house. Several years later, when he goes to sell the house, he is astonished to find out there is a $2,400 lien against John Shelby that affects his house.

Voluntary liens are deliberately placed by the owners, generally with their signatures. Examples of these are mortgages, second mortgages, and financing statements.

Let us say that John and Jackie Smith live in Rochester. Rochester has two major businesses, the Big Clinic and IBM. Suppose IBM decides to move its Rochester plant out of the country. Suddenly, there are many homes for sale in Rochester. The law of supply and demand would suggest that the value of John and Jackie's house would plummet.

John works for IBM and needs a new job. Because the value of their home is now less than the remaining balance on their mortgage, John and Jackie decide not to make payments. Once they quit making payments, their lender decides to foreclose. (The concept is the same for those who have overmortgaged a home and whose home value has dropped.)

Upon foreclosure, the bank sells the house for less than the mortgage amount. The bank has a deficiency. Under the terms of the mortgage and promissory note (i.e., a promise to repay the full loan amount), the bank sues John and Jackie for the difference. The bank obtains a "deficiency judgment" against John and Jackie for the shortage. While their mortgage was a specific lien, the deficiency judgment against John and Jackie is a general lien and, when filed in Rochester County, can be attached to both real and personal property that John and Jackie still own in Rochester County.

Involuntary liens, on the other hand, attach without the will and consent of the owner, by operation of law, statute, or court order. The deficiency judgment above against John and Jackie is involuntary.

> Discussion: In the scenario above, John and Jackie bought their home by assuming an existing mortgage from Sam and Lucille. Sam and Lucille's real estate agent, Frank, helped his sellers to negotiate a novation of the mortgage note and mortgage deed/deed of trust. *Novation* is the legal substitution of one party for another. Therefore, John and Jackie qualified for Sam and Lucille's mortgage, and the lender had them sign a new mortgage

note, returning Sam and Lucille's original mortgage note to them with a release of liability. What position would Sam and Lucille be in without novation?

■ Types of Liens

Remember, assuming there is enough money, liens can be paid off. If there is a dispute about a lien, money can be held in escrow (usually one and one-half times the lien amount) for the lien until the problem is resolved. If a lien creditor cannot be found, money can be escrowed or it can be paid into the court system to obtain a release.

Attorney's Lien

An *attorney's lien* is a lien filed by an attorney for services rendered. It is unusual in that it can be classified as either an involuntary, general, or specific lien because the attorney can file it either against a name or against real estate.

Status. This is NOT ACCEPTABLE; it needs to be released. Attorney's liens are most often seen in conjunction with judgments, a divorce, and/or bankruptcy.

Financing Statement

A *financing statement* is a document indicating that *personal property*, or *fixtures*, are encumbered with debt. It is the equivalent of a mortgage, but on personal property. Title companies do not generally look for financing statements, because they do not insure personal property as a rule. Financing statements matter to a real estate agent because, if there is a significant amount of personal property involved in a sale such as a large estate with a significant number of furnishings, there may be money owing. Or you may have a commercial building such as a hotel where the purchase agreement includes tens of thousands of dollars in restaurant equipment, beds, televisions, dressers, tables, chairs, and so on. All of the items being sold as part of the transaction may have been financed with money owing to the creditor at closing. If you are dealing with significant amounts of personal property, talk to the attorney or title company about looking for financing statements. Financing statement searches are done "by request." Endorsements to cover significant personal property are sometimes negotiated.

Status. Generally, if a financing statement shows up, it is ACCEPTABLE and can be paid, pursuant to the terms of the purchase agreement.

Mechanics' Liens and Materialmen's Liens

Mechanic's lien law says that if a contractor or subcontractor has supplied material or labor to improve a property and has not been paid for it, the contractor or subcontractor can, or in some cases automatically do, obtain a lien against the property where the work was performed or material delivered.

Status. These VARY; they are generally ACCEPTABLE in states where mechanics' liens and materialmen's liens attach only after recording, and a release needs to be obtained if a lien has been filed. Mechanics' liens usually have a specific life span (often one year), by state statute, at which time they expire and no action is required.

These liens are generally NOT ACCEPTABLE in states where mechanics' liens and materialmen's liens attach *without* recording. In these states, they require special attention. Discuss this with the title company.

In most states, mechanics' liens follow the recording rule and are a matter of constructive notice. This means they would be located by checking the public record. In some states, however, mechanics' liens are an exception to the recording rule, and the lien begins *not when the lien is filed, but when work is begun*. In those states, contractors can file liens up to 120 days or more, after their work is complete, and the lien is *retroactive* to the date of first work, even though no lien is filed of record.

This is a serious problem for title insurers, who must ask the owners and contractors whether or not any material has been delivered and installed or labor performed on the premises in the recent past (e.g., in the last 120 days) for which payment has not been made. This is generally done by an affidavit, so that should the truth not be told, the title company can sue for damages in a court of law. It is one of the largest claims areas for title insurers. In addition to the affidavit, lien waivers are collected from the suppliers and subcontractors, showing they have been paid.

Mechanics' liens are a particular problem in new construction development areas, where huge amounts of money are involved, and a great deal of material and labor have been recently supplied, all creating lien rights. Think about it—we are asking the contractor to list all the subcontractors of labor and material to the property, how much money they are owed and how much they have been paid. If the contractor leaves a subcontractor off the list, the money goes into the contractor's pocket. Contractors actually have an incentive to lie!

Furthermore, there may be multiple suppliers of a service, and there is no way for the title company to check every lumber company, every window company, painting contractor, heating contractor, plumbing contractor, electrical contractor, and so on, to see if they have supplied material or labor to the premises. Mechanics' liens are among the most risky and costly claims for a title underwriter.

> Discussion: How do mechanics' liens attach in your state—upon filing of a notice or upon supplying of material and/or labor?

In the event a known mechanic's lien is in dispute, an escrow will be set up until the dispute is settled. Normally, the title company will hold an amount equal to one and a half or two times the lien until the mechanic's lien issue is resolved.

Comment. Because mechanics' liens are specific liens, attaching to the property that was improved, they cannot be released by an affidavit stating they are not the persons against whom the lien was filed.

Judgment Liens

A *judgment lien* is a court order issued against the debtor and in favor of the plaintiff for a specific amount of money at the conclusion of a lawsuit. Once recorded in the county records, it becomes a general lien on the debtor's property.

Judgment liens against sellers. Judgment liens against sellers are GENERALLY NOT ACCEPTABLE—a release of land from judgment, or satisfaction of judgment, needs to be filed.

Judgment liens against buyers. What if my buyers have liens against them? When purchasing real estate, judgment liens affect buyers based on state law. Let us say Juan Garcia has a judgment and a tax lien filed against him. In some states, when he purchases a new home, the general liens that are already filed against his name would attach to the land *as soon as he buys it*. Therefore, his new mortgage will be subject to the judgment and tax lien unless released. In other words, they need to be paid before he can buy.

In many other states, a buyer can get a specific type of mortgage called a **purchase-money mortgage** that does not allow prior liens against the buyer to attach to a newly purchased property, so long as all money borrowed goes into the purchase. In this case, the general liens are subordinate to the purchase-money mortgage but would not be subordinate when the buyer sells, obtains a second mortgage, or refinances. (The purchase-money mortgage must secure funds solely for the purchase of the property. The mortgage should be executed simultaneously with the deed, then judgment liens—except U.S. judgments, also known as Abstracts of Judgment, which must be released—and federal tax liens against the purchaser are generally subordinate. Purchase-money mortgages appear in the following states: Alabama, Arkansas, California, Colorado, Connecticut, the District of Columbia, Florida, Georgia, Idaho, Illinois, Indiana, Kansas, Maryland, Minnesota, Mississippi, Missouri, Montana, Nebraska, New Jersey, New York, North Carolina, North Dakota, Ohio, Oklahoma, Oregon, Pennsylvania, South Carolina, South Dakota, Tennessee, Utah, Virginia, West Virginia, Wisconsin, and Wyoming.)

Problem. With releases, notice the language: "release *of land* from judgment." Say that our seller has a $50,000 judgment against him. He wishes to sell his property, legally described as Lot 1, Block 1, Blackacre. He is able to negotiate a $5,000 *partial* payment of judgment with the creditor to obtain a release. If he obtained a "partial release of judgment," the lot would *still* be encumbered, but with the remaining $45,000 judgment. By obtaining a "release *of land* for Lot 1, Block 1, Blackacre," the lot is no longer encumbered, but the remaining $45,000 balance on the judgment continues to affect the rest of the property of the debtor.

Problem. What about the judgments and use of affidavits? Because a general lien is filed against a person's name, and there are many people with the same or similar names, it is important to determine the identity of the judgment debtor. This is often handled by an affidavit of identity (sometimes called an "affidavit of non-identity").

An affidavit is somewhat self-serving because the debtor may be motivated to lie about the fact that he or she owes a large debt. While the affidavit will make an effort to obtain information, such as addresses for the past ten years, and match it with the judgment information, if the customer lies, the title company is at risk. In the event the name is an unusual name, and/or the judgment is significantly large, the title company may require an affidavit from a third party explaining the circumstances.

For example, a person named Frank Dieter Meyerson has a $31,512 judgment against him. The judgment shows he lived at 1215 Mabel Street, Naples, FL. Our seller, also one Frank Dieter Meyerson, says the judgment is not him and will sign an affidavit. In checking the judgment we see that the debtor on the judgment lived at 1215 Mabel Street, Naples, FL, so the affidavit certainly looks suspicious.

In this case the title company may require an affidavit from the judgment creditor stating that he is not the same Frank Dieter Meyerson against whom it has the judgment, or one can be obtained from a third party knowing the facts.

In this particular case, the title company accepted an affidavit from the seller's attorney explaining that our seller, Frank Dieter Meyerson, is the son of another Frank Dieter Meyerson, who is the judgment debtor, and that our seller previously lived with his father at 1215 Mabel Street, Naples, FL. That made sense.

Problem. In a number of states, you will find the doctrine of "idem sonans," which is Latin for "identical sounding." It means that if a name is spelled differently, but pronounced the same, the judgment should be shown. That is why a judgment on "Jean Johnson" may be shown when your seller's legal name is Jeanne Johnnson or a judgment on Jon Smith is shown against your seller, John Smyth. Generally, an affidavit of nonidentity will clear this problem.

Judgments and homestead property. In many states, judgments cannot attach to a person's homestead. However, in a number of states there are two types of homestead. The first one, "homestead for tax purposes," means that a person has filled out a real estate tax form declaring property to be his or her homestead, and is receiving a reduced real estate tax bill. In some states, the owner must declare tax homestead every year. In other states, once filed, tax homestead continues in effect until the property is sold of record.

However, tax homestead is differentiated in many states from what may be referred to as "legal homestead." *Legal homestead* means that the party has gone to court, and the court has legally determined that the property is truly their legal homestead and thus exempt from judgments listed in the order. As proof, the court will provide a document called a "Declaratory Judgment." Title companies will vary on how they handle judgments on homestead property. On large judgments, the title underwriter may require a Declaratory Judgment. On small judgments, they may be willing to take a statement from the seller that the property is his or her homestead. Discuss this with your title company, but beware when a judgment debtor claims that his or her property is exempt from a judgment because it is his or her "homestead."

State Tax Liens

State tax liens are statutory government liens in favor of the State Department of Revenue. Contrary to popular belief, the state tax lien, which is often thought of as a "first lien," only attaches to a person's real estate upon recording in the county (or local recording office) where the debtor owns property.

Status. These are NOT ACCEPTABLE. A satisfaction or release of land must be obtained at or before closing.

Comment. Similar to judgments, the lien against the common name may or may not be the person in the title commitment, and affidavits are routinely given to clarify names. Efforts are also made to match address and Social Security numbers when available, although under various privacy acts, these are less and less available.

Federal Tax Liens

These are statutory government liens in favor of the Internal Revenue Service. Contrary to popular belief, where federal tax liens are thought of as a "first lien," they also only attach to a person's real estate upon recording in the county (or local recording office) where the debtor owns property.

Status. These are NOT ACCEPTABLE. Obtain a full release or release of land from the Internal Revenue Service.

Comment. Similar to judgments, a federal tax lien against a common name may, or may not, be the person in the title commitment, and affidavits are routinely taken to clarify names. Efforts are also made to match Social Security numbers when available, although again, under various privacy acts, these are less and less available.

Child Support Liens

These are government liens, filed against a parent for nonpayment of child support and are generally payable to the Department of Health and Human Services where filed. A certified copy of child support liens can be refiled in any county in the United States to obtain lien rights where the debtor lives. To receive child support lien money, it is important to file where the debtor owns property.

Status. These are NOT ACCEPTABLE and must be paid, or an affidavit of nonidentity must be obtained, stating that the debtor is another person and there are no child support liens owing by the buyer or seller.

Federal District Court Judgments

These are judgment awards coming out of a federal district court. Normally, these types of cases have to do with *major, national* lawsuits and major national companies. Cases against tobacco companies, drug companies, automobile manufacturers, and so on, are likely to be filed and sued here. Because of the types of cases and the national impact, the judgments tend to have enormous awards.

Status. These are NOT ACCEPTABLE. Obtain a full release or partial release of land from the judgment creditor.

Comment. It is unlikely that you will run into these with an individual. Judgments tend to be against large national corporations. Similar to other judgments, however, a federal district court judgment could appear against a common name of a person who may, or may not be, the person in title. Affidavits are routinely taken to clarify nonidentity.

■ Red Flag Title Problems

When items shown below are on your title commitment, it will likely cause a delay in your closing unless they are recognized early and receive special attention to resolve them. These are much less common than the items shown above and they need particular consideration.

Bankrupt and Bankruptcy

A *bankrupt* is a person who through a court proceeding is relieved from payment of her or his debts, after surrendering her or his assets to the court appointed trustee. *Bankruptcy* is the court proceeding.

Status. Bankruptcy is NOT ACCEPTABLE and is very complicated. Discuss with the title company if the bankrupt is in fact your buyer or seller, and whether or not it has been discharged or is still valid.

Comment. An affidavit of nonidentity will suffice if the bankrupt listed on the title work is not your buyer or seller, but consult your title company if there are any questions.

Cloud on Title

Cloud on title is a generic term with no concrete definition. This terminology generally means that there is a fact or question about title that impairs its marketability. Clouds come in numerous forms. Both the problem and resolution should be detailed in the title commitment, or the title company may simply ask for further information or clarification. A typical example might be a "stray deed," one that has been recorded against the property but does not fit into the chain of title. The deed may have an erroneous description, or the party may have a legitimate interest, but some type of legal clarification is necessary. Most items listed above would be considered clouds on title until resolved.

Problem. This is NOT ACCEPTABLE. Discuss the particulars with the title company.

Homestead Exemption

A law that protects a portion of the value of an owner's principal residence from unsecured creditors, the homestead exemption is often claimed by a person with judgments as a defense for not paying the judgments. See "Judgment Liens" previously discussed.

Status. A homestead exemption requires special attention. Discuss it with the title company because the rules vary by state. The handling of the exemption will also vary from title company to title company.

Comment. Remember that homesteading a property for real estate taxes may *not* be the same as a legal homestead, which requires a court order called a "declaratory judgment." See "Judgment Liens" previously discussed.

Eminent Domain

All levels of government—federal, state, county, and municipal—have the right to take property or easements at any time when needed for the public good, with due process and provision of just compensation, through a court proceeding known as condemnation of lands. Generally, this has to do with widening a road or obtaining an easement, and the owner has little choice in the matter.

Status. Eminent domain problems require special attention. Discuss them with the title company.

Comment. Generally, there is nothing you can do about eminent domain. Eminent domain starts when a Notice of Lis Pendens has been filed, which is a document stating that there is pending litigation. (Lis pendens is discussed on page 54.) It states the government's intent to take property. For example, say a document shows the city wants to take the north five feet of the property for purposes of widening Main Street under its right of eminent domain. That information will show on the title commitment. The property can still close if the buyer is advised of its status, and agrees to accept the notice as an exception to the title policy. (The individuals involved still have the right to contest the issue and the right to compensation until the condemnation is complete.)

Abstract of Judgment in Favor of United States

This is a judgment in favor of the United States or any U.S. government agency—the lien is a general lien and is effective for 20 years. It must be paid by buyers as well because it does not qualify for exemption under a purchase-money mortgage. These judgments can be refiled for an additional 20 years.

Status. This is NOT ACCEPTABLE, it must be paid, or an affidavit of nonidentity must be given.

Pollution Control Liens

These liens are placed by various government agencies—federal, state, city, county, township, and so on—for pollution cleanup. The lien can be a specific lien or a general lien, because it may be filed against the party causing the pollution and/or against a specific parcel of land where pollution has contaminated a site.

Status. Pollution control liens are NOT ACCEPTABLE. Talk to your title company. Depending on the lien, the site may need to be cleaned up, which can be very expensive. In some cases, the pollution control agency may have already cleaned up the site and may file the lien against the owner to recoup the costs of the cleanup. If the lien is a general lien an affidavit of nonidentity may resolve the problem.

However, if the lien is a specific lien—that is, a lien against the land—the owner must clean up the property. There are cases where a lender has not foreclosed a mortgage, because foreclosure would put the lender in title, and the lender would then be responsible for cleanup costs in excess of the mortgage amount. If the owner and lender quit paying taxes, the property would eventually go tax forfeit, leaving the cleanup to the government.

Decree of Dissolution

The *decree of dissolution*, or divorce decree, is a court order dissolving a marriage and, frequently, splitting assets.

Status. The decree of dissolution requires special attention. Discuss the details with the title company.

Problem. The court will often include a number of issues in a decree of dissolution affecting title to the real estate. It may

- transfer title to one of the parties;
- create a lien in favor of the petitioner, respondent, or others in the decree;
- grant a name change for one or both of the parties;

- put stipulations in the document about the sale (such as not occurring until the children reach the age of majority); or
- put in numerous other special conditions and stipulations.

The title commitment will outline what needs to be done for the closing if there is a divorce decree. While both marriages and divorces that occur within the United States are recognized nationally, marriages and divorces that occur outside the United States may not be recognized, including those of servicemen and servicewomen. If you are aware of this situation, talk to your title company. It is also important to note that *state* law mandates the transfer of real estate. Therefore, if John Doe and Mary Doe, husband and wife, are divorced in California but own real estate in Wisconsin, a Wisconsin court will have to dispose of the Wisconsin real estate.

Comment. Title companies want an original certified copy of the decree of dissolution. Parties in a divorce have been known to alter and fax phony copies of a decree in order to avoid liens, creating significant title problems.

Comment. If your sellers are *not* getting along due to a messy divorce or if the new girlfriend or boyfriend plans to attend closing, please let the attorney or closer know! Former spouses can always be separated in different rooms to make the closing go more smoothly.

Notice of Lis Pendens (NLP)

A **notice of lis pendens (NLP)** is a generic term meaning a lawsuit has been filed in court and is pending on a specific parcel of property. Lis pendens is Latin for "pending litigation." NLPs are used for notice of any pending lawsuit—foreclosure of mortgages, widening of streets, taking of easements, perfecting of judgments or mechanics' liens, quiet title actions, and so on.

The term encompasses virtually all lawsuits.

Status. This is NOT ACCEPTABLE and a red flag that will very possibly delay closing.

Problem. It will likely be necessary to obtain and record a discharge of notice of lis pendens (in some states known as a "certificate of dismissal") from all lien claimants. A notice of lis pendens is a serious problem and generally must be resolved before or at closing. Depending on the reason for the lawsuit, its complexity, and the number of parties involved, it may be possible to escrow funds and still close. However, if the notice of lis pendens claims an interest in the property due to an unrecorded but valid document, for example, closing cannot occur until the lawsuit is resolved in a court of law, or the lawsuit is discharged.

Impact Fee

An impact fee is charged by a government agency when a new neighborhood is being developed by a builder. It is a tax used to offset expenses for such things as new roads, need for additional parks and schools, and additional sewer/water systems. It is most often paid by the builder as part of the sales price of the property but is negotiable.

■ Summary

The title commitment outlines the procedure for closing the transaction. By understanding the layout of the commitment, interested parties can get a quick handle on information. By understanding the most common title exceptions, an agent or lender can quickly determine the status of the property for closing and help customers understand what they are purchasing, what easements and restrictions affect the land, what issues need to be resolved before closing, and why.

Title insurance is involved in the vast majority of real estate transactions. It is key to closing a transaction (and getting paid). It is key to being sure your customers know what they are *really* buying—not only "the yellow house on Main Street next to the lake," but also the easements, restrictions, rights, and obligations that go with the property. By reviewing title work with them, you show yourself to be a truly competent agent or broker who has their best interests in mind.

case study

You have just received the title commitment for the biggest sale of your life! You have prepared a purchase agreement for Bill Gates on the most beautiful 40-acre piece of vacant property in the county, a $10 million sale!

You know Mr. Gates wishes to build a very large residential/commercial structure in a particular spot overlooking the lake. He intends to have large numbers of people at the home on a regular basis for fundraisers. You also are aware that the city is known for being difficult to work with when approving changes in zoning regulations and in dealing with new construction.

The title commitment shows the following nine items:

1. Title is in the names of John C. Banks and Elizabeth L. Banks, husband and wife, as joint tenants.
2. There are unpaid current real estate taxes in the amount of $34,526.
3. There are unpaid levied assessments in the amount of $124,516.
4. There is an upcoming hearing for a possible pending assessment.
5. The property is vacant land, and a standard owner's policy will be given in the amount of $10 million to The Bill & Melinda Gates Foundation.
6. Three easements are shown with long metes-and-bounds descriptions, one for a road, one for utilities, and one of which is a wetlands easement.
7. A "Developers Agreement with the City of Beaver Creek" includes an "impact fee" tax of 2½ percent of the sales price.
8. A lengthy set of restrictive covenants is filed on the land.
9. A state tax lien in the amount of $4,596.50 is filed against one "John Banks."

Mr. Gates will be calling you from his Seattle home tomorrow to get your "take" on the title work. What do you need to find out to respond appropriately to this incredible new customer?

Discussion Questions

1. What items shown on title work need additional research?
2. What information does title work provide on building codes?
3. What information does title work provide on local zoning rules?

Review Questions

1. The document that reflects all of the title research done and that is used to prepare closing documents is
   a. Schedule A.
   b. Schedule B.
   c. an endorsement.
   d. the commitment.

2. The effective date, how sellers currently hold title, and precise legal descriptions are shown on
   a. Schedule A.
   b. Schedule B-1.
   c. Schedule B-2.
   d. Schedule C.

3. The "meat" of the title policy, containing exclusions specific to the property, are shown on
   a. Schedule A.
   b. Schedule B.
   c. Schedule C.
   d. Schedule D.

4. The title commitment is generally good only for
   a. 30 days.
   b. 60 days.
   c. six months.
   d. any number of days until closed.

5. Exceptions to coverage that you will rarely find on title commitments are
   a. easements.
   b. mortgages.
   c. encroachments.
   d. assessments.

6. The most common easement found on properties is
   a. utility and drainage.
   b. blanket easement.
   c. driveway.
   d. access.

7. Another possible name for a second mortgage/deed of trust is a
   a. personal property lien.
   b. financing statement.
   c. home equity line of credit.
   d. mobile home lien.

8. A court proceeding relieving someone from payment of his or her debts is
   a. bankruptcy.
   b. judgment and decree.
   c. quiet title suit.
   d. notice of lis pendens.

9. A generic term referring to impaired marketability is
   a. cloud on title.
   b. bad title.
   c. quiet title.
   d. noisy title.

10. The tool most frequently used to show that judgments are not required to be paid at closing is the
    a. deed of trust.
    b. bankruptcy.
    c. affidavit of nonrecord matters.
    d. affidavit of nonidentity.

11. The government right used when property is needed for the public good is
    a. escheat.
    b. encumbrance.
    c. encroachment.
    d. eminent domain.

12. The term that means "pending litigation," a red flag for closing, is
    a. conclusions of law.
    b. notice of action.
    c. judgment and decree.
    d. notice of lis pendens.

chapter five

Understanding Title Policies

learning objectives

After completing this chapter, you will be able to

- list the two primary types of title policies and cite differences between them;
- recognize and explain the various parts of a title policy;
- discuss insurance coverage on the Homeowner's Policy of Title Insurance (Revised 1-1-2008); and
- explain coverage on the Extended Lender's Policy (Revised 1-1-2008).

Key Terms

conditions
covered risks
duty to defend
endorsements
exclusions
Expanded Coverage Residential Loan Policy
extended coverage
Homeowner's Policy of Title Insurance
Schedule A
Schedule B
subrogation

Obtaining the Title Coverage You Want

Title policies across the United States changed dramatically in 2008, with a significant increase in the amount of coverage for both lenders and owners. Along with the increase in coverage came a long overdue simplification in the number of policies available. Now, for one- to four-family residential dwellings, there are only two recommended policies: the ALTA Homeowner's Policy (1-1-2008) and the Expanded Coverage Residential Loan Policy (1-1-2008). These same policies are written by all five major title insurance underwriters. The five underwriter families write more than 90 percent of all title insurance in the United States. This means there is very little difference in title insurance coverage, and title companies will need to compete almost entirely on service.

Figure 5.1 | Percentage of Business for Five Major Title Companies

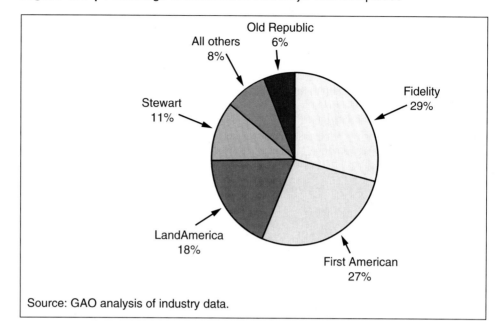

Source: GAO analysis of industry data.

However, even with the same exact policies available from almost all title underwriters, different title companies still deal with problems differently. What title Company A will insure, title Company B may not, based on their company's history and company policy. Some companies will specialize in niche markets—such as Indian lands, or oil and gas leases—that companies without expertise in those specific areas will not insure.

Just because one company turns you down does not mean you can't get the coverage your customer wants from another title company.

Marketable Title versus Insurable Title

Marketable title is different from insurable title. Marketable titles are free from reasonable doubt as to the interests held in the land, as determined by state law and by local custom. With marketable title, one clearly understands the ownership, rights, and interests in the land and there are no "clouds on title."

Insurable title, on the other hand, may technically be unmarketable and may have clouds on title. Title companies often take a calculated risk and insure over "unmarketable" titles. (Please note that some states make it *illegal* to insure unmarketable titles. In most states, however, it is acceptable. In all cases, the title insurance company will disclose any marketability issues on the title work.) To explain marketable title, let's say, for example, that we have a technical problem and need a release from a former owner. The title problem is 29 years and 10 months old. In this case, we know there is a legal statute of limitations that does not allow someone to claim an interest in real estate after 30 years. Technically, the title is still unmarketable, but the title company may accept it as an insurable risk, knowing that the problem will resolve itself in only two months.

Be aware that title companies insure titles differently. For instance, because title policies insure legal access as a standard part of the policy, a title without access is normally uninsurable until access is obtained. However, while one company may refuse to insure the title, another title company may be willing to insure the title if the purchaser is willing to take title knowing he or she has no legal access. The title company would likely have the buyer sign a "Notice of Title Defect" form showing lack of access for the parcel to protect itself, and would put a specific exception on the policy for access.

The salability of real estate is yet another issue. It is unrelated to marketability or insurability. For example, swampland can have marketable, insurable title, but nobody wants to buy it. Similarly, contamination of land alone does not affect marketability but may well affect its value and its salability. Title insurance does not cover salability.

Consumers should know they can shop a title company. If you have a title problem that one title company can't seem to resolve to your satisfaction, you would be wise to "shop" the issue to another title company, who may provide a more favorable response or at least give you some new options. Be sure, however, to explain problems to the shopped title company, as title insurance does not cover items known to the insured unless disclosed to the title insurer.

The Two Primary Policy Types—Lender's and Owner's

The lender's policy and the owner's policy are categorized by the party being insured. While there is a **standard policy** used for commercial properties and corporations, our discussion is limited to some of the highlights of the newest residential policies—the ALTA Expanded Coverage Residential Loan Policy (1-1-2008) and the ALTA Homeowner's Policy of Title Insurance for a One-to-Four Family Residence (1-1-2008). While not all title policies are ALTA policies (Texas has state-mandated forms, for example), ALTA policies are widely used and are representative of title policies nationally.

ALTA Title Policies Have Six Elements

All ALTA 2008 policy forms have the following six basic elements:

1. Covered risks
2. Duty to defend against legal action
3. Exclusions
4. Conditions
5. Schedule A
6. Schedule B—Exceptions

A number of standard endorsements, while not part of the basic policy, are frequently given to add significant supplementary coverage. A list of available endorsements is shown in Appendix Figure 4.

ALTA'S Homeowners Policy of Title Insurance for a One-to-Four Family Residence (1-1-2008)

Covered risks. The new 2008 owner's policy lists 32 specific covered risks. The covered risks include both general concepts of insurance and very specific insurance coverage. (See Appendix Figure 2 for a copy of the full terms and conditions of the homeowner's policy.) The policy should only be given on a one- to four-family improved residential site, and only when the insured owner is a "natural person" (human being or trustee of a trust).

The policy is quite thorough in examples of where titles might be bad. Some of the covered risks are:

- Someone else owns an interest in your title (other than as disclosed).
- Someone else claims to have rights affecting your title because of forgery or impersonation.
- A document on which your title is based is invalid because it was not properly signed, sealed, acknowledged, delivered, recorded, or indexed in the public records.
- Someone else has a lien on your title, including a
    - lien of real estate taxes or assessments imposed on your title by a governmental authority that are due or payable, but unpaid;
    - mortgage;
    - judgment, state, or federal tax lien;
    - charge by a homeowners' or condominium association; or
    - lien occurring before or after the policy date, for labor and material furnished before the policy date.
- An important coverage for all homeowners is legal access. The policy guarantees actual vehicular and pedestrian access to and from the land, based on a legal right. This does not mean physical access, but rather legal access. In other words, if the terrain requires that you fill a large hole to drive onto the property, but you have the legal right to access the property over the filled hole, you do not have a claim. However, if the only way you can access your house is by driving over a neighbor's lot to get to your house, the title policy would pay to obtain access.

Some survey issues—past, present, and future—are covered, and the new policy provides enhanced survey coverage. For example, the policy states it will cover a survey loss if

- you are forced to remove or remedy your existing structures, or any part of them—other than boundary walls or fences—because any portion was built without obtaining a building permit from the proper government office (subject to a stated deductible);
- you are forced to remove or remedy your existing structures, or any part of them, because they violate an existing zoning law or zoning regulation (subject to a stated deductible);
- you are forced to remove your existing structures because they encroach onto your neighbor's land (subject to a stated deductible);
- you are forced to remove your existing structures that encroach onto an easement or over a building setback line, even if the easement or building setback line is excepted in Schedule B; or
- your neighbor builds any structures *after* the policy date—other than boundary walls or fences—that encroach onto the land.

Duty to defend. The ALTA policy states, "We will defend Your Title in any legal action only as to that part of the action which is based on a Covered Risk and which is not excepted or excluded from coverage in this Policy. We will pay the costs, attorneys' fees, and expenses We incur in that defense." The insuring of marketability and paying expenses for defense are especially important elements to the policy for both the lender and owner. The cost of defending the title does not reduce the amount of insurance coverage. For example, you have a $350,000 owner's policy and have a title claim. If the title company spends $50,000 in legal fees on a lawsuit defending the claim on title but loses the lawsuit, they will still have to reimburse the insured the full $350,000.

Exclusions. The **exclusions** are a list of items that are not covered by the title policy. They are boilerplate language (i.e., the forms are preprinted and are the same for all properties). Exclusions for an owner's policy do not insure against loss, costs, attorney's fees, and expenses resulting from several general categories, including the rights of the government to enforce laws for health, safety, and welfare of the public; risks known or agreed to by the insured; bad funds; and rights to property outside or adjacent to the insured property. They read as follows:

1. Governmental police power, and the existence or violation of those portions of any law or government regulation concerning: building; zoning; land use; improvements on the land; land division; and environmental protection (except as provided)
2. The failure of your existing structures, or any part of them, to be constructed in accordance with applicable building codes (provides limited coverage in some cases)
3. The right to take the land by condemning it
4. Risks that are created, allowed, or agreed to by you, whether or not they are recorded in the public records; that are known to you at the policy date, but not to us, unless they are recorded in the public records at the policy date; that result in no loss to you; or that first occur after the policy date
5. Failure to pay value for your title
6. Lack of a right: to any land outside the area specifically described and referred to, and in streets, alleys, or waterways that touch the Land

Conditions. The **conditions** section of the policy outlines the contractual relationship between the insurance company and the insured. It includes such things as definitions, how to place a claim, and the rights and responsibilities of both the insured and the insurer. Key points include the following:

- The insured must provide proof of loss and has a duty to cooperate with and provide all relevant information to the title insurer to resolve title problems.
- The insurer has the right to choose the attorney when bringing or defending a legal action on your behalf and can appeal any decision to the highest level. They do not have to pay your claim until the legal action is finally decided and all appeals exhausted.
- The insurer has the right to pursue litigation as it deems appropriate, or to pay, or otherwise settle the claim. The insurer has a number of options pertaining to claims, including:
    - Pay the claim or pay the insured the amount due under the policy
    - Negotiate a settlement
    - Bring or defend a legal action related to the claim
    - Work out cures to the title with claimants, such as purchase a deed or release to clear title

A title company may insure over the problem again. Often a length of time will take care of a problem. For example, a missed judgment may be good for a period of ten years. By waiting for the ten years to run, the problem may be resolved.

The title company may also buy the loan from the lender and/or buy the property from the owner.

In one claims case, a title company missed a small "chicken scratch" designation on a subdivision map where new houses were being built. The "chicken scratch" was a marked designation in the key on the plat as a label for "Wetlands, as designated by the DNR." Not knowing about the wetlands, families bought, moved in, sodded their back yards, and improved them with built-in barbeques, swing sets, and so on. Later, the DNR required that these areas be restored to their original "wetlands" condition. The title company, having missed the designation, had a number of title claims and resolved the issue by buying back the houses. It then restored the wetlands, and resold the houses, clearly explaining the DNR wetlands easement this time.

Some enhancements to the 2008 owner's policy include:

- **Temporary housing coverage.** Interestingly enough, similar to car insurance that will allow a rental car if your car is incapacitated, the new title policy states: " [I]f You cannot use the Land because of a claim covered by this Policy: You may rent a reasonably equivalent substitute residence and We will repay You for the actual rent You pay, until the earlier of the cause of the claim is removed; or We pay You the amount required by this Policy. ... We will pay reasonable costs You pay to relocate any personal property You have the right to remove from the Land, including transportation of that personal property for up to twenty-five (25) miles from the Land, and repair of any damage to that personal property because of the relocation."
- **Policy amount increased up to 150 percent.** A big plus for the consumer is that the policy amount purchased will increase by 10 percent each year for the first five years following the policy date up to 150 percent of the original policy amount. The increase each year will happen on the anniversary of the policy date (shown in Schedule A).

Other key points in conditions include the following:

- **Subrogation.** Whenever the insurer is settling a claim, the insured owner/lender agrees to *transfer* legal rights to the title company to defend title. This means the insurer (who is now substituted for the owner/lender) can attempt to recover its loss in a court of law. If successful, the title insurer will keep the money obtained from the lawsuit. This transfer of rights prevents the insured from collecting both from the title company and again from the party causing the loss. This transfer of legal rights is called **subrogation.**
- **Arbitration.** Either party may demand arbitration if there is a title problem and the policy is $1,000,000 or less. If the policy is over $1,000,000, both parties must agree to arbitration. Arbitration is binding on both parties.

Schedule A. *Schedule A* states the what and who of the policy. Schedule A specifies the

- issuing title insurance company (e.g., title agency),
- policy number and amount,
- effective date and time through which the policy was written,

- deductible amounts, if any,
- exact names of the insureds,
- particular estate insured (e.g., fee simple),
- manner of vesting of title (e.g., a single person), and
- legal description of the property.

It often contains other information such as a tax parcel identification number or property address.

Schedule B. *Schedule B* generally carries over all exceptions to title that have not been removed from the title commitment at the time of closing. How exceptions to title are handled will vary. However, in most instances, the title company will accept some form of satisfactory evidence, such as inspections, surveys, or affidavits from the buyers and sellers in order to delete certain **standard exceptions**. The four most common "standard exceptions" are mechanics' liens; parties in possession; survey; and gap (time frame between the title commitment and date of closing). When standard exceptions are deleted, this is known as **extended coverage.** The 2008 policies provide extended coverage that is important for buyers.

All other issues pertaining to the specific parcel, such as the name of the new buyer, the buyer's new mortgage information, and remaining easements and restrictions would then be shown on Schedule B.

ALTA'S Expanded Coverage Residential Loan Policy (1-1-2008)

The new loan policy is very similar in its expanded coverage to the homeowner's policy. It has the same six key parts and policy forms have the following basic elements: covered risks, duty to defend, exclusions, conditions, Schedule A, and Schedule B. It also covers specific issues pertaining to the mortgage lending institution. Notable in each section for the lender are the following items:

Covered risks:

- The invalidity or unenforceability of the lien of the insured mortgage on the title
    - The lack of priority of the lien of the insured mortgage on the title over any other lien or encumbrance
    - The failure of the land
        - to have the street address shown in Schedule A, and the failure of the map, if any, attached to this policy to show the correct location and dimensions of the land according to the public record;
        - to be improved with a one- to four-family residential structure or, if stated in the description of the land, a residential condominium unit;
        - to be zoned to permit a one- to four-family residential structure or, if stated in the description of the land, a residential condominium unit; and
        - to be a lawfully created one- to four-family residential parcel according to state statutes and local ordinances governing subdivision of land.

- Forgery after the date of policy of
    - any instrument purporting to subordinate, assign, release, or reconvey the insured mortgage, and
    - any instrument purporting to convey or encumber the title.

Conditions:

- The policy says "In the event of any litigation…the Company shall have no liability for loss or damage until there has been a final determination by a court of competent jurisdiction, and disposition of all appeals, adverse to the Title or to the lien of the Insured Mortgage, as insured." The time taken to resolve title issues is a serious problem for the lender, particularly in a foreclosure market, when title problems most frequently appear. In plain language, if a title problem appears when a lender has taken a property in foreclosure, the lender has to hold the property until the problem is resolved. Because the title company has the right to appeal to disposition of all appeals, it could take years to resolve before having to fork over funds and holding property as REO (real estate owned by the lender), which is a very expensive proposition.
- If the company pursues its rights under Section 5 of these conditions (to clear title) and is unsuccessful in establishing the title or the lien of the insured mortgage, as insured, the amount of insurance shall be increased by 10 percent.
- The insurer has rights of subrogation against a lender's collateral. The policy stipulates that the title insurer has the right to go against any guarantees, indemnities, other policies of insurance, or bonds that a lender may be holding to insure its mortgage in order to recoup its title losses. A good example might be a builder that puts up additional collateral in the form of personal indemnities. If the builder then has unpaid mechanics' liens, the title company can go against the builder's personal indemnity to try to recoup its losses.
- All arbitrable matters when the amount of insurance is $2,000,000 or less will be arbitrated at the option of either the company or the insured. All arbitrable matters when the amount of insurance is in excess of $2,000,000 will be arbitrated only when agreed to by both the company and the insured.

Exclusions. Again, the exclusions are generally similar to the homeowner's policy but also cover issues pertaining to loan policies and the lender's responsibility. Specifically, the policy excludes coverage due to

- inability or failure of an insured to comply with applicable doing-business laws of the state where the land is situated, and
- inability or failure of an insured to comply with applicable usury or any consumer credit protection or truth-in-lending law.

Endorsements. Endorsements to the title policy can be used to delete exceptions or coverage or to add to or modify the policy. There are a number of common endorsements used for both an owner's policy and a lender's policy, including condominium endorsements; planned unit development endorsements; zoning endorsements; and restriction, encroachment, and mineral endorsements. There are also a variety of endorsements, for various types of mortgages, such as adjustable-rate mortgages or negative amortization mortgages. (See Appendix Figure 4 for a list of ALTA endorsements.)

In some instances, endorsements can be the most important part of a title policy, specifically crafting the policy to cover such things as air rights, water rights, and mineral rights, or giving special coverage against known title problems. On commercial properties in particular, policies are often endorsed to cover special needs such as parking easements or even personal property. These endorsements would be neogtiated with the insured or on an as-needed basis.

Summary

The two most current types of residential title policies are the Extended Lender's Policy of Title Insurance (1-1-2008) and the Homeowner's Policy of Title Insurance (1-1-2008). These policies should only be given on a one- to four-family improved residential site, and only when the insured owner is a "natural person" (human being or trustee of a trust). They are extended coverage policies, used across the United States, and are significantly better for the consumer, covering past, present, and some future title issues. Both of these title policies have six basic elements. First, the covered risks explain what insurance coverage is given. Second, the duty to defend clause explains that the insurer is obligated to defend any claim against title, legitimate or not. Third, the exclusions explain what coverage is not given. The conditions section outlines the contractual relationship between the insurance company and the insured. Schedule A states what and who are being insured. Schedule B, the key part of the policy, lists any exceptions to title that have not been removed, such as the current mortgage, unpaid taxes, easements, and restrictions. Endorsements, which occur frequently, can significantly modify the policy by deleting standard exceptions or greatly extending coverage.

case study

Mr. and Mrs. Jacobson located a wooded five-acre parcel of land adjacent to a small lake on which to build their dream home. The parcel was owned by the next-door neighbor, a semiretired builder named Henry Garth. Henry walked through the woods with them to show them the perimeter of the site, explaining that he personally had subdivided the land to "lay out each lot, in a somewhat irregular manner, according to the rolling terrain" so each lot would have access to the lake. He explained that all of the utility easements were five feet along each lot line and said all of the parcels in the neighborhood were exactly five acres because of the minimum zoning requirement from the city.

The Jacobsons decided to have Henry construct their home. He knew the property well and had subcontractors he had dealt with for years. He finished the house quickly and to the satisfaction of the Jacobsons.

The Jacobsons were paying cash for the rambler and decided to protect themselves with an owner's policy of title insurance. The title company examined title, finding Henry Garth in title. The inspector who examined the property could find no survey stakes, but Henry was there to show him the lot lines. When closing time came, everything went smoothly and the Jacobsons received their extended coverage homeowner's policy.

Several years later, after Henry had passed away, the Jacobsons decided to add to their garage. They contacted another local builder. The builder agreed to do the work and had the property surveyed to be sure the addition would fall within the lot lines. Much to the Jacobsons' distress, the survey showed that the existing house was actually two and one-half feet over on Henry's property. The Jacobsons contacted their title company with the problem.

Their 2008 extended title policy covered the following issues for the Jacobsons. Answer the questions following each issue.

The encroachment of the house onto the five-foot utility easement.

1. The extended policy coverage that insured the problem is
    a. parties in possession.
    b. survey.
    c. mechanic's lien issues.
    d. gap.

Needing to purchase two and one-half feet of Henry's property.

2. The extended policy coverage that insured the problem is
    a. parties in possession.
    b. survey.
    c. mechanic's lien issues.
    d. gap.

Probate of Henry's estate to buy the land.

3. This issue
    a. was covered by the title policy.
    b. was not covered by the title policy.

Rearrange lot lines.

4. The title company also needed to rearrange the lot lines to meet the five-acre minimum lot size required by the city.
    a. True
    b. False

Vacating five-foot easement under house.

5. The title company needed to vacate and possibly move the utility easement under the building.
    a. True
    b. False

Review Questions

1. What insures that a legal right of access to and from the land exists?
   a. Conditions
   b. Exclusions
   c. Covered risks
   d. Schedule A or B

2. Which section of the policy outlines the contractual relationship between the insurance company and the insured?
   a. Covered risks
   b. Exclusions
   c. Conditions
   d. Schedule A or B

3. What is the list of items shown on the policy jacket that are not covered by any title policy?
   a. Covered risks
   b. Exclusions
   c. Conditions
   d. Schedule A or B

4. Which states what and who are being insured and the type of policy?
   a. Insuring provisions
   b. Exclusions from coverage
   c. Conditions and stipulations
   d. Schedule A or B

5. What section describes the name of the insured and policy amount?
   a. Schedule A
   b. Schedule B
   c. Conditions
   d. Covered risks

6. Government rights fall under which of the following sections?
   a. Covered risks
   b. Exclusions
   c. Conditions
   d. Schedule A

7. What is the "meat of the title" as it pertains to the specific parcel being insured?
   a. Covered risks
   b. Exclusions
   c. Conditions
   d. Schedules A and B

8. Which is used to delete exceptions or coverage, or to modify the policy?
   a. Exclusions from coverage
   b. Eminent domain
   c. Encroachments
   d. Endorsements

9. What assures title to the estate or interest is as described in Schedule A?
   a. Covered risks
   b. Exclusions
   c. Conditions
   d. Schedule A or B

10. All 2008 homeowners' and extended loan policies insure that
    a. there are no liens or encumbrances on the title except as shown in the policy.
    b. you cannot lose possession of the property.
    c. there is physical access to and from the land.
    d. any physical additions you added to your own property have been paid for.

11. What one title company refuses to insure, another title company may be willing to insure.
    a. True
    b. False

chapter six

Title Insurance Requires Professionals

learning objectives

After completing this chapter, you will be able to

- place in chronological order the title insurance process that leads to closing and to the issuing of a title policy;
- describe the duties of the key players in a title office and know the player to contact for assistance; and
- identify reasons why it is critical to provide complete and accurate purchase agreement information to a title company in order to have a successful closing.

■ Key Terms

closing in escrow
HUD-1
name searches
state statutes/state laws
survey or inspection/plat drawing
table fund closing
title plant
Title Standards
underwriting manuals

Insuring title is a process involving *many* complex steps. The title insurance industry is comprised of a group of highly skilled real estate professionals who assist buyers, sellers, real estate agents, lenders, builders, and attorneys with the sale of all types of real estate properties, handling billions of dollars monthly.

■ Steps in the Title Insurance Process

> In real estate it is often said "location, location, location!" In title insurance it is often said "accuracy, accuracy, accuracy!"

Real estate title insuring is a complex process. Similar to a real estate agent's process in helping buyers and sellers close the transaction, there are numerous steps that must take place in order to complete the title transaction. The work flows generally as described in the following sections.

Order Processors

Order processing staff or an attorney will obtain important information from the purchase agreement and the title order to begin the process. They will

- verify addresses and legal descriptions;
- order tax and assessment information;
- order lien searches on buyers/sellers;
- look for previous files on the property;
- arrange for a **survey or inspection/plat drawing;**
- request a search on the chain of title—perhaps in the form of an abstract of title, or by having employees search a title plant to acquire copies of the original documents creating the chain of title or work from an existing title policy; and
- obtain a copy of a subdivision map or section map.

The accuracy of work in the order entry process is critical to obtaining title work. After all, if the legal description or names are incorrect, title work may be done on the wrong property!

For a real estate agent, attorney, or lender, providing complete, clear, and accurate information is critical to having a successful closing. Purchase agreements define how title is taken, how documents are to be prepared for the mortgage/deed of trust, and what the costs are charged to the buyers and sellers. For the closing, the purchase agreement is a fundamental document, providing a blueprint for the transaction. The most critical task for a real estate agent to achieve an excellent closing is to write a true, correct, complete, and accurate purchase agreement. The purchase agreement should represent the exact wishes, the "meeting of the minds," the "reality of consent" of your buyers and sellers. A thoughtful completion of the purchase agreement is essential to a great closing that will avoid problems such as the following:

- Leaving off information as to how the buyers wish to take title, for instance, "as joint tenants," "as tenants by the entireties," "as tenants in common," or under the "Phoebe Filibuster revocable trust agreement dated January 5, 2005," will require the attorney or closer to make calls to obtain the information so that he or she can prepare the correct legal documents.
- Misspellings in the names or use of nicknames for the buyers' legal name can create havoc, as can leaving out middle names or initials on a very common name, creating extra work, affidavits, and recording fees.
- Incorrect addresses will likely result in incorrect tax information, assessment information, and surveys.
- A full legal description rather than "legal to govern." In spite of the fact that it is in common use, some states have determined that the purchase agreement is unenforceable in a court of law unless it has a good legal description. After all, an address does not define lot size or location.
- Having "Michael Diaz" sign a purchase agreement as seller, without explaining that he is the personal representative of the estate of Tony Wilson, will create a flurry of phone calls and possibly a host of additional paperwork that might have been unnecessary had the purchase agreement been properly filled out.

■ Title Searchers

> If you want a good closing, present a good purchase agreement. No one wants to fix errors at the closing table! Your buyers and sellers may not remember the rest of the transaction, but they will remember the closing and how it went. And to a large extent they will attribute the success (or lack of success) of the closing to their real estate agent.

"Abstractors" or "title searchers" are professionals who hunt for the history of title or "chain of title" based on the public records. In many states, this requires a special state license. The search may be done from the public record or from an internal **title plant** maintained by the title company, which is a reorganization of the county's records into grantor-grantee books, or geographical tracts (by legal description) for purposes of searching. Title plants often also contain records from other offices such as court records, bankruptcy, probate, and other documents.

Most of the 3,141 counties in the United States maintain real estate records by a system of grantor and grantee. (Counties occur in 48 states as a local level of government. Parishes occur in Louisiana, and boroughs are used in parts of New York and in Alaska. *www.fact-index.com/c/co/county__united_states_.html*) This means that records are kept by the name of the sellers and buyers. In searching this type of index, the task can become overwhelming when searching by name. Think for example of John Smith, James Anderson, or Sergio Garcia, all common in different parts of the country. When searching names like these, there will likely be many people with the same or similar names whose records have nothing to do with the property in question.

The title search is reasonably complex. The title searcher or abstractor must be familiar with how each recording office maintains its records. This means knowing the system of how to search in the offices of the treasurers, auditors, assessors, recorders, district courts, circuit courts, federal courts, and other public offices (i.e., how to locate deeds, mortgages/deeds of trust, miscellaneous records, grantor and grantee indices, probate records, and various other types of legal documents). It means knowing state statutes and customs of the local attorneys. When records do not "fit together," the abstractor must be creative in finding ways to make the pieces of the puzzle fit into a chain of title. That might mean locating a divorce decree or name change, or finding probate papers because the seller is deceased.

In many states "abstracts of title" are prepared. These are typed "books" that provide a summary of all of the pertinent information the title searcher has obtained. The abstract shows a condensed version of each document recorded in the public record against a particular piece of land from the "patent," or "land grant," the original government conveyances, to the most current date available. The abstract also includes tax and assessment information, and **name searches** (for general liens such as state tax liens, federal tax liens, and judgments or bankruptcies, that are filed against any person with the same name, or even possibly a similar name to a person chain title). It includes documents filed against the real estate, such as an easement, a restriction, a mortgage, or a mechanic's lien. The abstract is a cost-effective way of maintaining a complete chain of title as it is passed down from seller to buyer, over and over again, each time the title is transferred. In many areas, a shortened version of an abstract is completed for each transaction.

In other areas, a "title search" package is prepared. This consists of searching the same records as mentioned above and providing actual copies of the documents for the attorney or examiner to review. A title search package is not passed down from seller to buyer but is reconstructed each time a property is sold, based on existing title evidence. So, if a title company has recently worked on a property, they will not need to recreate their former work, but can search from that date forward.

The abstract or title search is a key segment in the process of insuring title. Obviously, accuracy is critical to the title policy. If documents are not properly located, the title company might miss a judgment, mortgage/deed of trust, mechanic's lien, easement, and so on, that would cause a serious claim on the policy, loss to the title underwriter, and possibly loss of the property to the owner.

■ Title Examiners

The *title examiner* receives, reviews, and evaluates the critical pieces of information provided by the abstractor, including the following:

- The purchase agreement and any other information provided by the agent
- The title insurance application or order from the real estate agent, lender, or attorney
- The abstract or an old title policy with the current title search
- Tax and assessment information
- The survey or inspection/plat drawing (see Appendix Figure 7 for a sample copy of an inspection/plat drawing)

Examiners are highly skilled in real estate, being able to correctly draw and identify complex legal descriptions. Their careful examination assures that the legal description is correct and a good "chain of title" exists. Where problems exist, they identify them and set them forth in the commitment to insure.

Examiners must be familiar with real estate law. This means being familiar with **state statutes/state laws** and *case law*, which are in constant flux, changing each time the legislature meets, or a new court case is determined. Recognize too that state statutes might have case law in opposition, which must be considered! Requirements on the title commitment represent calculated risks as figured by the title examiner with the help of a title underwriter in complex cases.

Examiners must know practices common to the local bar associations, who frequently publish **Title Standards.** Title Standards are generally accepted principles agreed on by each local (state) bar association. They give guidance as to what technical problems create a reasonable doubt about the quality of title. Title Standards, while in common practice in most states, are just guidelines and although they are not law, they do affect what is generally accepted as "marketable title," meaning title that is free from reasonable doubt as to claims.

In addition to this, the examiner must know practices and procedures as set forth in the **underwriting manuals,** which are guidelines set forth by their title underwriter. And they must know the terms of the legal contract between the title agent and his or her underwriter. For example, many underwriters have a maximum policy amount (such as $1 million) that can be written by a title agent without review by the underwriter. This limits the underwriter's liability. Underwriting manuals are provided by the insurer to assist in resolving common title issues, set forth company policy, and to provide standard language for use in a title policy or commitment to insure. In sticky situations, or situations with unusual risks, the written approval of the underwriter is required. This is where various title underwriters disagree, and a host of companies may handle the same sticky title problem differently.

> The underwriter's determination is based on claims history and on what they deem appropriate for the marketplace. There is no solid consensus of opinion on examining or underwriting. What one underwriter always refuses to insure, another underwriter often agrees to insure.

In preparing the title commitment, the examiner verifies buyer and seller names; validates the correct legal description, addresses, and so on; makes note of liens affecting the property, including mortgage/deeds of trust or deeds of trust, assessment liens, and any general liens or bankruptcies against the buyer, seller, or previous owners. He or she checks each document looking for appropriate signatures and proper acknowledgments, reviewing the validity of each document in the chain of title.

Examiners also search for evidence of forgery or possible fraud. (Was the sellers' mortgage paid off the week *before* closing?) They look to see that all prior encumbrances have been released and that all prior interests in the property have been properly conveyed. They review the purchase agreement information as to the names of the sellers and buyers, terms of financing to be insured, whether an owner's policy is desired, and so on. They also review information received about survey issues and any visual inspections performed on the property. These items assist in removing standard exceptions as to parties in possession, survey, mechanics' liens, and so on.

The examiner then identifies all requirements that must be taken care of at closing and lists items that will remain on the policy as exceptions to title. These carefully drawn conclusions about the status of title generate the "title commitment" (also known as title binder). The title commitment is the key document that shows the complete status of title (as of the *effective date*, that is, a given day and time). It is the insurer's offer to insure the property, subject to the items shown and the payment of premium.

In order to protect the customer, a real estate agent should obtain a copy and understand the title commitment. That means looking at title work before closing, getting copies of documents if needed, and asking questions if something is not understood. After all, if your buyers have a title problem, you have a title problem. Remember, your buyers are counting on you to coach them through this transaction.

■ Attorney/Closer/Closing Assistant

Closers are the individuals who pull all the pieces together for the actual legal transfer of the property. In some states, the closer must be an attorney or supervised by an attorney. In other states, paralegals perform closings. To complete the transaction successfully, they must deal with a number of pieces, including the following:

- *Purchase agreement.* (This is also known as the earnest money contract or sales contract.) This provides information to the closer as to what is being purchased, names of the buyers, what documents need to be drawn, the sales price, earnest money, anticipated terms of any mortgage/deed of trust financing, and so on, and is arguably the most important document at closing. It is the blueprint for the closing.
- *Lender's instructions.* The lender provides a comprehensive list of instructions for each closing. These may include instructions to the closer to obtain proof of payoff of loans, proof of sale of a previous home, or a host of other items. It specifies the lender's fees, includes a list of items to be obtained such as truth-in-lending forms, proof of homeowners' hazard insurance, and the type of mortgage to be executed. In many cases, a lender will also have "master

closing instructions" that are detailed instructions, designed to provide closers with rules or guidelines as to how to handle that particular lender's files.

- *VA/FHA/FNMA/FHLMC guidelines.* Closers are also responsible for knowing general rules of the VA, FHA, FNMA, or FHLMC in order to craft appropriate documents and prepare an accurate **HUD-1** closing statement. The HUD-1 is the U.S. Department of Housing and Urban Development settlement statement, which is required on any residential transactions using VA, FHA, FNMA, or FHLMC loans.

  A HUD-1 closing statement is not required on commercial or cash sales.

- *Title commitment.* The title commitment gives a set of requirements for documents that need to be obtained. The title commitment is broken down into the two key sections already discussed. Schedule A sets forth the interest to be insured, the name of the insured, the amount of the insurance, the legal description of the property, and property address, and Schedule B sets forth exceptions to the policy. The commitment will show all known interests in the real estate that a buyer or lender would wish to know. The closer is responsible for reviewing all documents in order to properly remove all requirements from the title commitment for a clean title policy, and for creating new documents.

What you, the real estate agent, see as "the closing" is only a small portion of a closer's responsibilities. Prior to the closing, there are many hours of preparation—preparing documents, obtaining pay-off figures on mortgages and liens, creating a comprehensive closing statement, clearing title objections, talking with buyers, sellers, attorneys, title examiners, real estate agents, lenders, and so on, in order to fund the loan and close the transaction.

The closing itself is the consummation of the transaction. It may be **closing in escrow** where title agents handle the closing details without the buyers and sellers meeting face to face. In this case, documents pour in over a period of time, and when all conditions of the closing are met, the closer records documents and disburses funds. Or it may be a **table fund closing,** where everyone involved sits down at the closing table together to complete the transaction.

A table fund closing is a very powerful event. Here documents are received, explained, and signed. Money is accepted from the buyers and the lender and is disbursed to the sellers; the sellers' mortgage company; the real estate agent; the buyers' new lender; any lien claimants; and others. This closing may last only an hour or so, but it is a very important event in the process. An event most buyers and sellers will remember for a long time. It is an event that will often determine if the buyers and sellers will return to you for their next transaction or will look for another lender or agent. People remember their closing.

After the closing, there are more hours of work as the process continues, and many follow up items need to be accomplished. An original mortgage/deed of trust, the note, the HUD-1 statement, truth-in-lending forms, and numerous other documents must be returned to the lender along with their fees. Checks must be sent to pay off the seller's mortgages and any other liens. Satisfactions or releases must be obtained on each item and sent for recording to the proper public office. Packages of documents are sent to the county recorder, clerk of court, or other authority to create legal notice of changes. Taxes and assessments must be paid, and title policies must be prepared and sent out to lenders and/or owners. Copies of all documents are maintained for due diligence and proof that conditions were met, as well as for title underwriter or government audits.

It takes a special kind of person to be a first-rate closer. This person must be very detail-oriented. She or he must carefully review contracts and create corresponding new legal documents, being extremely cautious not to miss important information from the purchase agreement, the lender's instructions, the title work, or recording requirements. To protect the title company, a closer should be bonded. After all, the closer handles millions of dollars each month. Besides all this, the closer must deal with the high-strung emotions of the buyers and sellers who not only are leaving their old homes to move on to new ones but are also making the biggest financial commitment of their lives. The closer must be trustworthy, professional, personable, comforting, and friendly, and must provide a sense of well-being, order, and confidence that all is well. This is not a job for just anyone.

Recording Specialists

Many title companies retain "recording specialists" or use a vendor management company to record documents, because of the complexity of different recording offices. Each recording office will have a list of requirements as to how the documents have to be prepared to be recordable in their respective office along with a list of fees for recording that is specific to their county, city, state, or court. Typically, there will also be government documents, such as a certificate of value or a transfer declaration that discloses the sale price to the local assessor. These are often used to evaluate the fair market value of a home for tax purposes. Real estate taxes must be paid. There might be environmental documents, such as a well disclosure if well water is used or located on the property. And the county and/or state will require special fees, such as deed tax, mortgage/deed of trust tax, conservation fees, impact fees, recording fees, and a host of other fees that vary from state to state, county to county, or city to city. A recording specialist's job involves a complex recording system intertwined with the treasurer, auditor, county recorder, and various courts. And of course, time is of the essence because documents recorded first in time are first in right.

Other Title Company Personnel

Many other professionals are needed to keep the title business running efficiently. While we will not examine their job descriptions, the following deserve mention and are critical to managing the business and customer service:

- *Marketing staff* work to bring in new business and assist existing customers with training, events, and special requests.
- *Customer service* handles general information, answering customer questions, and frequently opens new files to start a transaction. Customer service personnel deal with special requests and often handle the transaction post-closing when customers need a copy of their closing statement for tax purposes, for example.
- *Record keeping* maintains closed title files for the following: future reference—as the property will eventually be sold again; legal purposes—policies written are legal contracts where claims information will be critical; state and federal regulations—ensuring that truth-in-lending forms and RESPA requirements have been met; HUD-1 statements properly prepared and money disbursed according to the statement; along with records pertaining to the due diligence requirements of the underwriter. It also means knowing and complying with new privacy laws such as the Gramm-Leach-Bliley Act.

- *Title plant personnel* maintain copies of daily records that come from a host of locations so that the title company can have a complete set of records pertaining to title. In some states, having a private title plant is a state requirement for a title company. As we have discussed, many companies are now sending these jobs overseas to India, China, and the Philippines in order to lower costs.
- *Claims and legal, human resources, accounting, policy preparation,* and *management* are all essential for the day-to-day success of the business.

Summary

As you can see, the title company is about accuracy, accuracy, accuracy. It takes a number of skilled, professional people to help real estate professionals move from the purchase agreement through the transaction to closing. As a professional who wants a successful closing, you need to know the key title players involved in transitioning your sale through to closing. An important part of this process is the agent or broker providing a thorough, complete, and accurate purchase agreement for the title company. For a lender it means providing complete and accurate closing instructions. For the title company, it means employing competent and trustworthy personnel.

The other key role for an agent, broker, or lender is reviewing the title work with the understanding of what it means in order to meet the customers' needs and passing the information to the buyer. Title companies work with many parties to make closings go as smoothly as possible.

case study

The listing agent has been in the real estate business for three weeks. Unbeknownst to you, he has been dealing with an attorney, Frederick Hampton, Esquire, who represented Buckmeister Fuller, owner of the property being sold, and now deceased. The listing agent provided the multiple listing service records with Mr. Hampton as the owner and lists the property with an address of 312 Pleasant Lake Road, and legal description of Block 3, Lot 2, Lake Addition.

In fact, Mr. Fuller's heirs now own the property. The address is 213 Pleasant Lake Drive, and the legal description is Lot 3, Block 2, Pleasant Lake 1st Addition.

Because the purchase agreement was written according to the multiple listing service, title work was done on the wrong property. The closing is scheduled for tomorrow at 3 PM. The closer calls you to ask a few questions. When you realize what has happened, you tell the closer that title work will have to be redone.

1. Who will the title company need to coordinate to redo the title work for tomorrow's closing?
    a. Order processing staff, closer, accounting
    b. Title searchers, title examiner, claims
    c. Title examiner, closer, recording specialist, inspector
    d. Order processing, inspector, title searcher, title examiner, closer

2. What additional or corrective information does the title company need to get the title work right?

Review Questions

1. Put the following in chronological order.
   a. Title searcher
   b. Order processor
   c. Recording specialist
   d. Closer

2. Put the following in chronological order.
   a. Policy department
   b. Title examiner
   c. Closer
   d. Abstractors

3. Whom do you call for technical questions on clearing title on a title commitment?
   a. Title searcher
   b. Title examiner/attorney
   c. Recording specialist
   d. Closer

4. Whom do you call for general training?
   a. Order processor
   b. Marketing
   c. Recording specialist
   d. Human resources

5. Who determines if sticky title exceptions can be insured over?
   a. Marketing
   b. Claims
   c. Underwriter
   d. Order processor

6. Whom would you call to locate a copy of the HUD-1 closing statement 18 months after the file was closed?
   a. Claims
   b. Order processor
   c. Underwriter
   d. Record keeping

7. Whose job is it to locate judgments and state and federal tax liens in the public record?
   a. Claims
   b. Order processor
   c. Abstractor/searcher
   d. Title examiner

8. Whose job is it to create HUD-1 closing statements?
   a. Marketing
   b. Abstractors
   c. Recording specialist
   d. Closer

9. When title agents handle the closing details without meeting the buyers and sellers face to face, it is known as
   a. table funding.
   b. closing.
   c. closing in escrow.
   d. HUD-1.

10. Who is responsible for knowing the general rules of the VA, FHA, FNMA, or FHLMC, so that the loan can be sold on the secondary market?
    a. Lender
    b. Closing assistant
    c. Closer
    d. All of the above

11. The key document, post-closing, that shows the complete status of title (as of a certain day and time), is the
    a. endorsement.
    b. binder or commitment.
    c. policy.
    d. exclusions to coverage.

Title Insurance Forms and Samples

appendix

Appendix Figure 1 | Notice of Availability of Owner's Title Insurance

---

American Land Title Association

Notice of Availability of Owner's Title Insurance
1978
Section VI-1

BLANK TITLE INSURANCE COMPANY

NOTICE OF AVAILABILITY OF OWNER'S TITLE INSURANCE

To:_____   Date:_____

_____

Buying property identified as:_____

_____

    A Mortgagee's Policy of title insurance insuring the title to the property you are buying is being issued to your mortgage lender, but that policy does not provide title insurance coverage to you.

    You may obtain an Owner's Policy of title insurance which provides title insurance coverage to you. The additional cost to you for an Owner's Policy of title insurance in the amount of $____ is $____, if you request it at this time.

    If you are uncertain as to whether you should obtain an Owner's Policy of title insurance, you are urged to seek independent advice.

_____

(Show name of entity providing notice)

_____ I/We do request an Owner's policy of title insurance.

_____ I/We do not request an Owner's Policy of title insurance.

    Date:_____   Buyer:_____

                                      Buyer:_____

Appendix Figure 2 | ALTA Homeowner's Policy

American Land Title Association

Homeowner's Policy
Revised 1/01/08

HOMEOWNER'S POLICY OF TITLE INSURANCE
FOR A ONE-TO-FOUR FAMILY RESIDENCE

Issued By

BLANK TITLE INSURANCE COMPANY

OWNER'S INFORMATION SHEET

Your Title Insurance Policy is a legal contract between You and Us.

It applies only to a one-to-four family residence and only if each insured named in Schedule A is a Natural Person. If the Land described in Schedule A of the Policy is not an improved residential lot on which there is located a one-to-four family residence, or if each insured named in Schedule A is not a Natural Person, contact Us immediately.

The Policy insures You against actual loss resulting from certain Covered Risks. These Covered Risks are listed beginning on page of the Policy. The Policy is limited by:

- Provisions of Schedule A
- Exceptions in Schedule B
- Our Duty To Defend Against Legal Actions On Page ___
- Exclusions on page ___
- Conditions on pages ___ and ___.

You should keep the Policy even if You transfer Your Title to the Land. It may protect against claims made against You by someone else after You transfer Your Title.

IF YOU WANT TO MAKE A CLAIM, SEE SECTION 3 UNDER CONDITIONS ON PAGE ___.

The premium for this Policy is paid once. No additional premium is owed for the Policy.

This sheet is not Your insurance Policy. It is only a brief outline of some of the important Policy features. The Policy explains in detail Your rights and obligations and Our rights and obligations. Since the Policy--and not this sheet--is the legal document,

YOU SHOULD READ THE POLICY VERY CAREFULLY.

If You have any questions about Your Policy, contact:

BLANK TITLE INSURANCE COMPANY
_____
_____

Appendix Figure 2 | ALTA Homeowner's Policy (continued)

American Land Title Association	Homeowner's Policy
	Revised 1/01/08

HOMEOWNER'S POLICY OF TITLE INSURANCE
FOR A ONE-TO-FOUR FAMILY RESIDENCE

Issued By

BLANK TITLE INSURANCE COMPANY

<u>TABLE OF CONTENTS</u>

    PAGE

OWNER'S COVERAGE STATEMENT —

COVERED RISKS —

OUR DUTY TO DEFEND AGAINST LEGAL ACTIONS —

EXCLUSIONS —

CONDITIONS
1. Definitions —
2. Continuation of Coverage —
3. How to Make a Claim —
4. Our Choices When We Learn of a Claim —
5. Handling a Claim or Legal Action —
6. Limitation of Our Liability —
7. Transfer of Your Rights to Us —
8. This Policy is the Entire Contract —
9. Increased Policy Amount —
10. Severability —
11. Arbitration —
12. Choice of Law —

SCHEDULE A —
    Policy Number, [Premium], Date [and Time] and Amount
    Deductible Amounts and Maximum Dollar Limits of Liability
    Street Address of the Land
    1. Name of Insured
    2. Interest in Land Covered
    3. Description of the Land

SCHEDULE B -- EXCEPTIONS —

Appendix Figure 2 | ALTA Homeowner's Policy (continued)

American Land Title Association

Homeowner's Policy
Revised 1/01/08

HOMEOWNER'S POLICY OF TITLE INSURANCE
FOR A ONE-TO-FOUR FAMILY RESIDENCE

Issued By

BLANK TITLE INSURANCE COMPANY

As soon as You Know of anything that might be covered by this Policy, You must notify Us promptly in writing at the address shown in Section 3 of the Conditions.

OWNER'S COVERAGE STATEMENT

This Policy insures You against actual loss, including any costs, attorneys' fees and expenses provided under this Policy. The loss must result from one or more of the Covered Risks set forth below. This Policy covers only Land that is an improved residential lot on which there is located a one-to-four family residence and only when each insured named in Schedule A is a Natural Person.

Your insurance is effective on the Policy Date. This Policy covers Your actual loss from any risk described under Covered Risks if the event creating the risk exists on the Policy Date or, to the extent expressly stated in Covered Risks, after the Policy Date.

Your insurance is limited by all of the following:

- The Policy Amount
- For Covered Risk 16, 18, 19 and 21, Your Deductible Amount and Our Maximum Dollar Limit of Liability shown in Schedule A
- The Exceptions in Schedule B
- Our Duty To Defend Against Legal Actions
- The Exclusions on page
- The Conditions on pages   and   .

COVERED RISKS

The Covered Risks are:

1. Someone else owns an interest in Your Title.
2. Someone else has rights affecting Your Title because of leases, contracts, or options.
3. Someone else claims to have rights affecting Your Title because of forgery or impersonation.
4. Someone else has an easement on the Land.
5. Someone else has a right to limit Your use of the Land.
6. Your Title is defective. Some of these defects are:
    a. Someone else's failure to have authorized a transfer or conveyance of your Title.
    b. Someone else's failure to create a valid document by electronic means.
    c. A document upon which Your Title is based is invalid because it was not properly signed, sealed, acknowledged, delivered or recorded.

Appendix Figure 2 | ALTA Homeowner's Policy (continued)

American Land Title Association

Homeowner's Policy

Revised 1/01/08

    d. A document upon which Your Title is based was signed using a falsified, expired, or otherwise invalid power of attorney.

    e. A document upon which Your Title is based was not properly filed, recorded, or indexed in the Public Records.

    f. A defective judicial or administrative proceeding.

7. Any of Covered Risks 1 through 6 occurring after the Policy Date.

8. Someone else has a lien on Your Title, including a:

    a. lien of real estate taxes or assessments imposed on Your Title by a governmental authority that are due or payable, but unpaid;

    b. Mortgage;

    c. judgment, state or federal tax lien;

    d. charge by a homeowner's or condominium association; or

    e. lien, occurring before or after the Policy Date, for labor and material furnished before the Policy Date.

9. Someone else has an encumbrance on Your Title.

10. Someone else claims to have rights affecting Your Title because of fraud, duress, incompetency or incapacity.

11. You do not have actual vehicular and pedestrian access to and from the Land, based upon a legal right.

12. You are forced to correct or remove an existing violation of any covenant, condition or restriction affecting the Land, even if the covenant, condition or restriction is excepted in Schedule B. However, You are not covered for any violation that relates to:

    a. any obligation to perform maintenance or repair on the Land; or

    b. environmental protection of any kind, including hazardous or toxic conditions or substances

unless there is a notice recorded in the Public Records, describing any part of the Land, claiming a violation exists. Our liability for this Covered Risk is limited to the extent of the violation stated in that notice.

13. Your Title is lost or taken because of a violation of any covenant, condition or restriction, which occurred before You acquired Your Title, even if the covenant, condition or restriction is excepted in Schedule B.

14. The violation or enforcement of those portions of any law or government regulation concerning:

    a. building;

    b. zoning;

    c. land use;

    d. improvements on the Land;

    e. land division; or

    f. environmental protection,

if there is a notice recorded in the Public Records, describing any part of the Land, claiming a violation exists or declaring the intention to enforce the law or regulation. Our liability for this Covered Risk is limited to the extent of the violation or enforcement stated in that notice.

15. An enforcement action based on the exercise of a governmental police power not covered by Covered Risk 14 if there is a notice recorded in the Public Records, describing any part of the Land, of the enforcement action or intention to bring an enforcement action. Our liability for this Covered Risk is limited to the extent of the enforcement action stated in that notice.

Appendix Figure 2 | ALTA Homeowner's Policy (continued)

American Land Title Association
Homeowner's Policy
Revised 1/01/08

16. Because of an existing violation of a subdivision law or regulation affecting the Land:

    a. You are unable to obtain a building permit;

    b. You are required to correct or remove the violation; or

    c. someone else has a legal right to, and does, refuse to perform a contract to purchase the Land, lease it or make a Mortgage loan on it.

    The amount of Your insurance for this Covered Risk is subject to Your Deductible Amount and Our Maximum Dollar Limit of Liability shown in Schedule A.

17. You lose Your Title to any part of the Land because of the right to take the Land by condemning it, if:

    a. there is a notice of the exercise of the right recorded in the Public Records and the notice describes any part of the Land; or

    b. the taking happened before the Policy Date and is binding on You if You bought the Land without Knowing of the taking.

18. You are forced to remove or remedy Your existing structures, or any part of them - other than boundary walls or fences - because any portion was built without obtaining a building permit from the proper government office. The amount of Your insurance for this Covered Risk is subject to Your Deductible Amount and Our Maximum Dollar Limit of Liability shown in Schedule A.

19. You are forced to remove or remedy Your existing structures, or any part of them, because they violate an existing zoning law or zoning regulation. If You are required to remedy any portion of Your existing structures, the amount of Your insurance for this Covered Risk is subject to Your Deductible Amount and Our Maximum Dollar Limit of Liability shown in Schedule A.

20. You cannot use the Land because use as a single-family residence violates an existing zoning law or zoning regulation.

21. You are forced to remove Your existing structures because they encroach onto Your neighbor's land. If the encroaching structures are boundary walls or fences, the amount of Your insurance for this Covered Risk is subject to Your Deductible Amount and Our Maximum Dollar Limit of Liability shown in Schedule A.

22. Someone else has a legal right to, and does, refuse to perform a contract to purchase the Land, lease it or make a Mortgage loan on it because Your neighbor's existing structures encroach onto the Land.

23. You are forced to remove Your existing structures which encroach onto an easement or over a building set-back line, even if the easement or building set-back line is excepted in Schedule B.

24. Your existing structures are damaged because of the exercise of a right to maintain or use any easement affecting the Land, even if the easement is excepted in Schedule B.

25. Your existing improvements (or a replacement or modification made to them after the Policy Date), including lawns, shrubbery or trees, are damaged because of the future exercise of a right to use the surface of the Land for the extraction or development of minerals, water or any other substance, even if those rights are excepted or reserved from the description of the Land or excepted in Schedule B.

26. Someone else tries to enforce a discriminatory covenant, condition or restriction that they claim affects Your Title which is based upon race, color, religion, sex, handicap, familial status, or national origin.

27. A taxing authority assesses supplemental real estate taxes not previously assessed against the Land for any period before the Policy Date because of construction or a change of ownership or use that occurred before the Policy Date.

28. Your neighbor builds any structures after the Policy Date -- other than boundary walls or fences -- which encroach onto the Land.

Appendix Figure 2 | ALTA Homeowner's Policy (continued)

American Land Title Association

Homeowner's Policy
Revised 1/01/08

29. Your Title is unmarketable, which allows someone else to refuse to perform a contract to purchase the Land, lease it or make a Mortgage loan on it.

30. Someone else owns an interest in Your Title because a court order invalidates a prior transfer of the title under federal bankruptcy, state insolvency, or similar creditors' rights laws.

31. The residence with the address shown in Schedule A is not located on the Land at the Policy Date.

32. The map, if any, attached to this Policy does not show the correct location of the Land according to the Public Records.

OUR DUTY TO DEFEND AGAINST LEGAL ACTIONS

We will defend Your Title in any legal action only as to that part of the action which is based on a Covered Risk and which is not excepted or excluded from coverage in this Policy. We will pay the costs, attorneys' fees, and expenses We incur in that defense.

We will not pay for any part of the legal action which is not based on a Covered Risk or which is excepted or excluded from coverage in this Policy.

We can end Our duty to defend Your Title under Section 4 of the Conditions.

THIS POLICY IS NOT COMPLETE WITHOUT SCHEDULES A AND B.

[Witness clause optional]

BLANK TITLE INSURANCE COMPANY

BY:_____

PRESIDENT

BY:_____

SECRETARY

EXCLUSIONS

In addition to the Exceptions in Schedule B, You are not insured against loss, costs, attorneys' fees, and expenses resulting from:

1. Governmental police power, and the existence or violation of those portions of any law or government regulation concerning:

    a. building;

    b. zoning;

    c. land use;

    d. improvements on the Land;

    e. land division; and

    f. environmental protection.

    This Exclusion does not limit the coverage described in Covered Risk 8.a., 14, 15, 16, 18, 19, 20, 23 or 27.

2. The failure of Your existing structures, or any part of them, to be constructed in accordance with applicable building codes. This Exclusion does not limit the coverage described in Covered Risk 14 or 15.

3. The right to take the Land by condemning it. This Exclusion does not limit the coverage described in Covered Risk 17.

Appendix Figure 2 | ALTA Homeowner's Policy (continued)

American Land Title Association Homeowner's Policy
Revised 1/01/08

4. Risks:

    a. that are created, allowed, or agreed to by You, whether or not they are recorded in the Public Records;

    b. that are Known to You at the Policy Date, but not to Us, unless they are recorded in the Public Records at the Policy Date;

    c. that result in no loss to You; or

    d. that first occur after the Policy Date - this does not limit the coverage described in Covered Risk 7, 8.e., 25, 26, 27 or 28.

5. Failure to pay value for Your Title.

6. Lack of a right:

    a. to any land outside the area specifically described and referred to in paragraph 3 of Schedule A; and

    b. in streets, alleys, or waterways that touch the Land.

    This Exclusion does not limit the coverage described in Covered Risk 11 or 21.

Appendix Figure 2 | ALTA Homeowner's Policy (continued)

American Land Title Association
Homeowner's Policy
Revised 1/01/08

HOMEOWNER'S POLICY OF TITLE INSURANCE
FOR A ONE-TO-FOUR FAMILY RESIDENCE

Issued By

BLANK TITLE INSURANCE COMPANY

CONDITIONS

1. <u>DEFINITIONS</u>

   a. <u>Easement</u> - the right of someone else to use the Land for a special purpose.

   b. <u>Known</u> - things about which You have actual knowledge. The words "Know" and "Knowing" have the same meaning as Known.

   c. <u>Land</u> - the land or condominium unit described in paragraph 3 of Schedule A and any improvements on the Land which are real property.

   d. <u>Mortgage</u> - a mortgage, deed of trust, trust deed or other security instrument.

   e. <u>Natural Person</u> - a human being, not a commercial or legal organization or entity. Natural Person includes a trustee of a Trust even if the trustee is not a human being.

   f. <u>Policy Date</u> - the date and time shown in Schedule A. If the insured named in Schedule A first acquires the interest shown in Schedule A by an instrument recorded in the Public Records later than the date and time shown in Schedule A, the Policy Date is the date and time the instrument is recorded.

   g. <u>Public Records</u> - records that give constructive notice of matters affecting Your Title, according to the state statutes where the Land is located.

   h. <u>Title</u> - the ownership of Your interest in the Land, as shown in Schedule A.

   i. <u>Trust</u> - a living trust established by a human being for estate planning.

   j. <u>We/Our/Us</u> - Blank Title Insurance Company.

   k. <u>You/Your</u> - the insured named in Schedule A and also those identified in Section 2.b. of these Conditions.

2. <u>CONTINUATION OF COVERAGE</u>

   a. This Policy insures You forever, even after You no longer have Your Title. You cannot assign this Policy to anyone else.

   b. This Policy also insures:

      (1) anyone who inherits Your Title because of Your death;

      (2) Your spouse who receives Your Title because of dissolution of Your marriage;

      (3) the trustee or successor trustee of a Trust to whom You transfer Your Title after the Policy Date; or

      (4) the beneficiaries of Your Trust upon Your death.

   c. We may assert against the insureds identified in Section 2.b. any rights and defenses that We have against any previous insured under this Policy.

3. <u>HOW TO MAKE A CLAIM</u>

   a. <u>Prompt Notice Of Your Claim</u>

      (1) As soon as You Know of anything that might be covered by this Policy, You must notify Us promptly in writing.

      (2) (Send Your notice to **Blank Title Insurance Company**, , Attention: Claims Department. Please include the Policy number shown in Schedule A, and the county and state where the Land is located. Please enclose a copy of Your policy, if available.

Appendix Figure 2 | ALTA Homeowner's Policy (continued)

American Land Title Association
Homeowner's Policy
Revised 1/01/08

    (3) If You do not give Us prompt notice, Your coverage will be reduced or ended, but only to the extent Your failure affects Our ability to resolve the claim or defend You.

  b. Proof Of Your Loss

    (1) We may require You to give Us a written statement signed by You describing Your loss which includes:

      (a) the basis of Your claim;

      (b) the Covered Risks which resulted in Your loss;

      (c) the dollar amount of Your loss; and

      (d) the method You used to compute the amount of Your loss.

    (2) We may require You to make available to Us records, checks, letters, contracts, insurance policies and other papers which relate to Your claim. We may make copies of these papers.

    (3) We may require You to answer questions about Your claim under oath.

    (4) If you fail or refuse to give Us a statement of loss, answer Our questions under oath, or make available to Us the papers We request, Your coverage will be reduced or ended, but only to the extent Your failure or refusal affects Our ability to resolve the claim or defend You.

4. OUR CHOICES WHEN WE LEARN OF A CLAIM

  a. After We receive Your notice, or otherwise learn, of a claim that is covered by this Policy, Our choices include one or more of the following:

    (1) Pay the claim;

    (2) Negotiate a settlement;

    (3) Bring or defend a legal action related to the claim;

    (4) Pay You the amount required by this Policy;

    (5) End the coverage of this Policy for the claim by paying You Your actual loss resulting from the Covered Risk, and those costs, attorneys' fees and expenses incurred up to that time which We are obligated to pay;

    (6) End the coverage described in Covered Risk 16, 18, 19 or 21 by paying You the amount of Your insurance then in force for the particular Covered Risk, and those costs, attorneys' fees and expenses incurred up to that time which We are obligated to pay;

    (7) End all coverage of this Policy by paying You the Policy Amount then in force, and those costs, attorneys' fees and expenses incurred up to that time which We are obligated to pay;

    (8) Take other appropriate action.

  b. When We choose the options in Sections 4.a. (5), (6) or (7), all Our obligations for the claim end, including Our obligation to defend, or continue to defend, any legal action.

  c. Even if We do not think that the Policy covers the claim, We may choose one or more of the options above. By doing so, We do not give up any rights.

5. HANDLING A CLAIM OR LEGAL ACTION

  a. You must cooperate with Us in handling any claim or legal action and give Us all relevant information.

  b. If You fail or refuse to cooperate with Us, Your coverage will be reduced or ended, but only to the extent Your failure or refusal affects Our ability to resolve the claim or defend You.

  c. We are required to repay You only for those settlement costs, attorneys' fees and expenses that We approve in advance.

  d. We have the right to choose the attorney when We bring or defend a legal action on Your behalf. We can appeal any decision to the highest level. We do not have to pay Your claim until the legal action is finally decided.

Appendix Figure 2 | ALTA Homeowner's Policy (continued)

American Land Title Association	Homeowner's Policy
	Revised 1/01/08

    e. Whether or not We agree there is coverage, We can bring or defend a legal action, or take other appropriate action under this Policy. By doing so, We do not give up any rights.

6. LIMITATION OF OUR LIABILITY

    a. After subtracting Your Deductible Amount if it applies, We will pay no more than the least of:

    (1) Your actual loss;

    (2) Our Maximum Dollar Limit of Liability then in force for the particular Covered Risk, for claims covered only under Covered Risk 16, 18, 19 or 21; or

    (3) the Policy Amount then in force.

    and any costs, attorneys' fees and expenses that We are obligated to pay under this Policy.

    b. If We pursue Our rights under Sections 4.a.(3) and 5.e. of these Conditions and are unsuccessful in establishing the Title, as insured:

    (1) he Policy Amount then in force will be increased by 10% of the Policy Amount shown in Schedule A, and

    (2) You shall have the right to have the actual loss determined on either the date the claim was made by You or the date it is settled and paid.

    c. (1) If We remove the cause of the claim with reasonable diligence after receiving notice of it, all Our obligations for the claim end, including any obligation for loss You had while We were removing the cause of the claim.

      (2) Regardless of 6.c.(1) above, if You cannot use the Land because of a claim covered by this Policy:

        (a) You may rent a reasonably equivalent substitute residence and We will repay You for the actual rent You pay, until the earlier of:

          i. the cause of the claim is removed; or

          ii. We pay You the amount required by this Policy. If Your claim is covered only under Covered Risk 16, 18, 19 or 21, that payment is the amount of Your insurance then in force for the particular Covered Risk.

        (b) We will pay reasonable costs You pay to relocate any personal property You have the right to remove from the Land, including transportation of that personal property for up to twenty-five (25) miles from the Land, and repair of any damage to that personal property because of the relocation. The amount We will pay You under this paragraph is limited to the value of the personal property before You relocate it.

    d. All payments We make under this Policy reduce the Policy Amount then in force, except for costs, attorneys' fees and expenses. All payments We make for claims which are covered only under Covered Risk 16, 18, 19 or 21 also reduce Our Maximum Dollar Limit of Liability for the particular Covered Risk, except for costs, attorneys' fees and expenses.

    e. If We issue, or have issued, a Policy to the owner of a Mortgage that is on Your Title and We have not given You any coverage against the Mortgage, then:

    (1) We have the right to pay any amount due You under this Policy to the owner of the Mortgage, and any amount paid shall be treated as a payment to You under this Policy, including under Section 4.a. of these Conditions;

    (2) Any amount paid to the owner of the Mortgage shall be subtracted from the Policy Amount then in force ; and

    (3) If Your claim is covered only under Covered Risk 16, 18, 19 or 21, any amount paid to the owner of the Mortgage shall also be subtracted from Our Maximum Dollar Limit of Liability for the particular Covered Risk.

    f. If You do anything to affect any right of recovery You may have against someone else, We can subtract from Our liability the amount by which You reduced the value of that right.

Appendix Figure 2 | ALTA Homeowner's Policy (continued)

American Land Title Association

Homeowner's Policy

Revised 1/01/08

7. <u>TRANSFER OF YOUR RIGHTS TO US</u>

    a. When We settle Your claim, We have all the rights and remedies You have against any person or property related to the claim. You must not do anything to affect these rights and remedies. When We ask, You must execute documents to evidence the transfer to Us of these rights and remedies. You must let Us use Your name in enforcing these rights and remedies.

    b. We will not be liable to You if We do not pursue these rights and remedies or if We do not recover any amount that might be recoverable.

    c. We will pay any money We collect from enforcing these rights and remedies in the following order:

        (1) to Us for the costs, attorneys' fees and expenses We paid to enforce these rights and remedies;

        (2) to You for Your loss that You have not already collected;

        (3) to Us for any money We paid out under this Policy on account of Your claim; and

        (4) to You whatever is left.

    d. If You have rights and remedies under contracts (such as indemnities, guaranties, bonds or other policies of insurance) to recover all or part of Your loss, then We have all of those rights and remedies, even if those contracts provide that those obligated have all of Your rights and remedies under this Policy.

8. <u>THIS POLICY IS THE ENTIRE CONTRACT</u>

This Policy, with any endorsements, is the entire contract between You and Us. To determine the meaning of any part of this Policy, You must read the entire Policy and any endorsements. Any changes to this Policy must be agreed to in writing by Us. Any claim You make against Us must be made under this Policy and is subject to its terms.

9. <u>INCREASED POLICY AMOUNT</u>

The Policy Amount then in force will increase by ten percent (10%) of the Policy Amount shown in Schedule A each year for the first five years following the Policy Date shown in Schedule A, up to one hundred fifty percent (150%) of the Policy Amount shown in Schedule A. The increase each year will happen on the anniversary of the Policy Date shown in Schedule A.

10. <u>SEVERABILITY</u>

If any part of this Policy is held to be legally unenforceable, both You and We can still enforce the rest of this Policy.

11. <u>ARBITRATION</u>

    a. If permitted in the state where the Land is located, You or We may demand arbitration.

    b. The law used in the arbitration is the law of the state where the Land is located.

    c. The arbitration shall be under the Title Insurance Arbitration Rules of the American Land Title Association ("Rules"). You can get a copy of the Rules from Us.

    d. Except as provided in the Rules, You cannot join or consolidate Your claim or controversy with claims or controversies of other persons.

    e. The arbitration shall be binding on both You and Us. The arbitration shall decide any matter in dispute between You and Us.

    f. The arbitration award may be entered as a judgment in the proper court.

12. <u>CHOICE OF LAW</u>

The law of the state where the Land is located shall apply to this policy.

Appendix Figure 2 | ALTA Homeowner's Policy (continued)

American Land Title Association — Homeowner's Policy
Revised 1/01/08

HOMEOWNER'S POLICY OF TITLE INSURANCE
FOR A ONE-TO-FOUR FAMILY RESIDENCE

Issued By

BLANK TITLE INSURANCE COMPANY

SCHEDULE A

Our name and address is: Blank Title Insurance Company
(Company Name)
(Company Address)

Policy No.: [Premium: $_____] Policy Amount: $ Policy Date [and Time]:

Deductible Amounts and Maximum Dollar Limits of Liability

For Covered Risk 16, 18, 19 and 21:

	Your Deductible Amount	Our Maximum Dollar Limit of Liability
Covered Risk 16:	% of Policy Amount Shown in Schedule A or $	$
	(whichever is less)	
Covered Risk 18:	% of Policy Amount Shown in Schedule A or $	$
	(whichever is less)	
Covered Risk 19:	% of Policy Amount Shown in Schedule A or $	$
	(whichever is less)	
Covered Risk 21:	% of Policy Amount Shown in Schedule A or $	$
	(whichever is less)	

Street Address of the Land:

1. Name of Insured:
2. Your interest in the Land covered by this Policy is:
3. The Land referred to in this Policy is described as:

Appendix Figure 2 | ALTA Homeowner's Policy (continued)

American Land Title Association	Homeowner's Policy
	Revised 1/01/08

HOMEOWNER'S POLICY OF TITLE INSURANCE
FOR A ONE-TO-FOUR FAMILY RESIDENCE

Issued By

BLANK TITLE INSURANCE COMPANY

SCHEDULE B

EXCEPTIONS

In addition to the Exclusions, You are not insured against loss, costs, attorneys' fees, and expenses resulting from:

Appendix Figure 3 | ALTA Loan Policy

American Land Title Association	Expanded Coverage Residential Loan Policy
	Revised 1/01/08

EXPANDED COVERAGE RESIDENTIAL LOAN POLICY
FOR A ONE-TO-FOUR FAMILY RESIDENCE

Issued By

BLANK TITLE INSURANCE COMPANY

Any notice of claim and any other notice or statement in writing required to be given to the Company under this Policy must be given to the Company at the address shown in Section 17 of the Conditions.

SUBJECT TO THE EXCLUSIONS FROM COVERAGE, THE EXCEPTIONS FROM COVERAGE CONTAINED IN SCHEDULE B, AND THE CONDITIONS, BLANK TITLE INSURANCE COMPANY, a Blank corporation (the "Company") insures as of Date of Policy and, to the extent stated in Covered Risks 11, 16, 17, 18, 19, 20, 21, 22, 23, 24, 27 and 28, after Date of Policy, against loss or damage, not exceeding the Amount of Insurance, sustained or incurred by the Insured by reason of:

COVERED RISKS

1. Title being vested other than as stated in Schedule A.

2. Any defect in or lien or encumbrance on the Title. This Covered Risk includes but is not limited to insurance against loss from

    (a) A defect in the Title caused by

    (i) forgery, fraud, undue influence, duress, incompetency, incapacity, or impersonation;

    (ii) failure of any person or Entity to have authorized a transfer or conveyance;

    (iii) a document affecting Title not properly created, executed, witnessed, sealed, acknowledged, notarized, or delivered;

    (iv) failure to perform those acts necessary to create a document by electronic means authorized by law;

    (v) a document executed under a falsified, expired, or otherwise invalid power of attorney;

    (vi) a document not properly filed, recorded, or indexed in the Public Records including failure to perform those acts by electronic means authorized by law; or

    (vii) a defective judicial or administrative proceeding.

    (b) The lien of real estate taxes or assessments imposed on the Title by a governmental authority due or payable, but unpaid.

    (c) Any encroachment, encumbrance, violation, variation, or adverse circumstance affecting the Title that would be disclosed by an accurate and complete land survey of the Land. The term "encroachment" includes encroachments of existing improvements located on the Land onto adjoining land, and encroachments onto the Land of existing improvements located on adjoining land.

3. Unmarketable Title.

4. 4. No right of access to and from the Land.

5. 5. The violation or enforcement of any law, ordinance, permit, or governmental regulation (including those relating to building and zoning) restricting, regulating, prohibiting, or relating to

    (a) the occupancy, use, or enjoyment of the Land;

    (b) the character, dimensions, or location of any improvement erected on the Land;

    (c) the subdivision of land; or

    (d) environmental protection

Appendix Figure 3 | ALTA Loan Policy (continued)

American Land Title Association   Expanded Coverage Residential Loan Policy

Revised 1/01/08

    if a notice, describing any part of the Land, is recorded in the Public Records setting forth the violation or intention to enforce, but only to the extent of the violation or enforcement referred to in that notice.

6. An enforcement action based on the exercise of a governmental police power not covered by Covered Risk 5 if a notice of the enforcement action, describing any part of the Land, is recorded in the Public Records, but only to the extent of the enforcement referred to in that notice.

7. The exercise of the rights of eminent domain if a notice of the exercise, describing any part of the Land, is recorded in the Public Records.

8. Any taking by a governmental body that has occurred and is binding on the rights of a purchaser for value without Knowledge.

9. The invalidity or unenforceability of the lien of the Insured Mortgage upon the Title. This Covered Risk includes but is not limited to insurance against loss from any of the following impairing the lien of the Insured Mortgage

    (a) forgery, fraud, undue influence, duress, incompetency, incapacity, or impersonation;

    (b) failure of any person or Entity to have authorized a transfer or conveyance;

    (c) the Insured Mortgage not being properly created, executed, witnessed, sealed, acknowledged, notarized, or delivered;

    (d) failure to perform those acts necessary to create a document by electronic means authorized by law;

    (e) a document executed under a falsified, expired, or otherwise invalid power of attorney;

    (f) a document not properly filed, recorded, or indexed in the Public Records including failure to perform those acts by electronic means authorized by law; or

    (g) a defective judicial or administrative proceeding.

10. The lack of priority of the lien of the Insured Mortgage upon the Title over any other lien or encumbrance.

11. The lack of priority of the lien of the Insured Mortgage upon the Title

    (a) as security for each and every advance of proceeds of the loan secured by the Insured Mortgage over any statutory lien for services, labor, or material arising from construction of an improvement or work related to the Land when the improvement or work is either

        (i) contracted for or commenced on or before Date of Policy; or

        (ii) contracted for, commenced, or continued after Date of Policy if the construction is financed, in whole or in part, by proceeds of the loan secured by the Insured Mortgage that the Insured has advanced or is obligated on Date of Policy to advance;

    (b) over the lien of any assessments for street improvements under construction or completed at Date of Policy;

    (c) over any defect in or lien or encumbrance on the Title attaching or created before, on or after Date of Policy; as to each and every advance of proceeds of the loan secured by the Insured Mortgage, which at Date of Policy the Insured has made or is legally obligated to make; and

    (d) over any environmental protection lien that comes into existence before, on or after Date of Policy pursuant to any federal statute in effect at Date of Policy as to each and every advance of proceeds of the loan secured by the Insured Mortgage, which at Date of Policy the Insured has made or is legally obligated to make.

12. The invalidity or unenforceability of any assignment of the Insured Mortgage, provided the assignment is shown in Schedule A, or the failure of the assignment shown in Schedule A to vest title to the Insured Mortgage in the named Insured assignee free and clear of all liens.

Appendix Figure 3 | ALTA Loan Policy (continued)

American Land Title Association   Expanded Coverage Residential Loan Policy

Revised 1/01/08

13. The failure of the Land

    (a) to have the street address shown in Schedule A, and the failure of the map, if any, attached to this policy to show the correct location and dimensions of the Land according to the Public Record .

    (b) to be improved with a one-to-four family residential structure or, if stated in the description of the Land, a residential condominium unit.

    (c) to be zoned to permit a one-to-four family residential structure or, if stated in the description of the Land, a residential condominium unit.

    (d) to be a lawfully created one-to-four family residential parcel according to state statutes and local ordinances governing subdivision of land.

14. The forced removal, modification or replacement of any existing one-to-four family residential structure or residential condominium unit located on the Land resulting from the violation of any of the following requirements of any applicable zoning ordinance: Area or dimensions of the Land as a building site; floor space area of the structure; height of the structure; or distance of the structure from the boundary lines of the Land.

15. The assessment or taxation of the Land by governmental authority as part of a larger parcel.

16. The failure of the existing one-to-four family residential structure or residential condominium unit or a portion or a future modification or replacement to have been constructed with a valid building permit from the appropriate local government issuing office or agency.

17. The inability to use the existing one-to-four family residential structure or residential condominium unit or a portion of it or a future modification or replacement to it for one-to-four family residential purposes because that use violates a restriction shown in Schedule B.

18. Damage to improvements, lawns, shrubbery or trees constructed or planted on the Land before, on or after Date of Policy resulting from the future exercise of any right to use the surface of the Land for the extraction or development of minerals, water or any other substance.

19. The encroachment onto the Land of an improvement constructed after Date of Policy.

20. Encroachment of improvements constructed on the Land after Date of Policy onto adjoining property or over any easement or building setback line on the Land.

21. Forgery after Date of Policy of

    (a) any instrument purporting to subordinate, assign, release or reconvey the Insured Mortgage; and

    (b) any instrument purporting to convey or encumber the Title.

22. The invalidity, unenforceability or lack of priority of the lien of the Insured Mortgage as to Advances made or changes in the rate of interest charged subsequent to any modification of the terms of the Insured Mortgage made after Date of Policy which are secured by the terms of the Insured Mortgage as modified.

23. Damage to improvements, lawns, shrubbery or trees constructed or planted on the Land before, on or after Date of Policy occasioned by the exercise of the right to use or maintain any easement referred to in Schedule B.

24. Interference with the use for one-to-four family residential purposes of the improvements constructed on the Land before, on or after Date of Policy occasioned by the exercise of the right to use or maintain any easement referred to in Schedule B.

25. Supplemental real estate taxes, including those caused by construction or a change of ownership or use, that occurred before Date of Policy, not previously assessed against the Land for any period before Date of Policy.

Appendix Figure 3 | ALTA Loan Policy (continued)

American Land Title Association	Expanded Coverage Residential Loan Policy
	Revised 1/01/08

26. The invalidity or unenforceability of the lien of the Insured Mortgage upon the Title based upon a violation of the usury laws of the state where the Land is located if no other Mortgage is shown as an exception in Schedule B.

27. The invalidity, unenforceability, lack of priority, or avoidance of the lien of the Insured Mortgage upon the Title

    (a) resulting from the avoidance in whole or in part, or from a court order providing an alternative remedy, of any transfer of all or any part of the title to or any interest in the Land occurring prior to the transaction creating the lien of the Insured Mortgage because that prior transfer constituted a fraudulent or preferential transfer under federal bankruptcy, state insolvency, or similar creditors' rights laws; or

    (b) because the Insured Mortgage constitutes a preferential transfer under federal bankruptcy, state insolvency, or similar creditors' rights laws by reason of the failure of its recording in the Public Records

        (i) to be timely, or

        (ii) to impart notice of its existence to a purchaser for value or to a judgment or lien creditor.

28. Any defect in or lien or encumbrance on the Title or other matter insured against by this Policy that has been created or attached or has been filed or recorded in the Public Records subsequent to Date of Policy and prior to the recording of the Insured Mortgage in the Public Records.

Unless stated to the contrary in Schedule B, the Company incorporates the following American Land Title Association endorsements into this policy by this reference as if these endorsements had been attached to this policy

(a) ALTA Form [4-06] [4.1-06] (Condominium), if a condominium unit is referred to in the description of the Land;

(b) ALTA Form [5-06] [5.1-06] (Planned Unit Development);

(c) ALTA Form 6-06 (Variable Rate Mortgage);

(d) ALTA Form 6.2-06 (Variable Rate Mortgage - Negative Amortization); and

(e) ALTA Form 8.1-06 (Environmental Protection Lien) subject to the statutes, if any, shown in Schedule B specifically for this endorsement.

(f) ALTA Form 9.3-06 (Restrictions, Encroachments, Minerals).

The Company will also pay the costs, attorneys' fees, and expenses incurred in defense of any matter insured against by this policy, but only to the extent provided in the Conditions.

[Witness clause optional]

BLANK TITLE INSURANCE COMPANY

BY: PRESIDENT

BY: SECRETARY

Appendix Figure 3 | ALTA Loan Policy (continued)

EXCLUSIONS FROM COVERAGE

The following matters are expressly excluded from the coverage of this policy and the Company will not pay loss or damage, costs, attorneys' fees or expenses which arise by reason of:

1. (a) Any law, ordinance, permit, or governmental regulation (including those relating to building and zoning) restricting, regulating, prohibiting, or relating to

   (i) the occupancy, use, or enjoyment of the Land;

   (ii) the character, dimensions, or location of any improvement erected on the Land;

   (iii) the subdivision of land; or

   (iv) environmental protection;

   or the effect of any violation of these laws, ordinances, or governmental regulations. This Exclusion 1(a) does not modify or limit the coverage provided under Covered Risk 5, 6, 13(c), 13(d), 14 or 16.

   (b) Any governmental police power. This Exclusion 1(b) does not modify or limit the coverage provided under Covered Risk 5, 6, 13(c), 13(d), 14 or 16.

2. Rights of eminent domain. This Exclusion does not modify or limit the coverage provided under Covered Risk 7 or 8.

3. Defects, liens, encumbrances, adverse claims, or other matters

   (a) created, suffered, assumed, or agreed to by the Insured Claimant;

   (b) not Known to the Company, not recorded in the Public Records at Date of Policy, but Known to the Insured Claimant and not disclosed in writing to the Company by the Insured Claimant prior to the date the Insured Claimant became an Insured under this policy;

   (c) resulting in no loss or damage to the Insured Claimant;

   (d) attaching or created subsequent to Date of Policy (however, this does not modify or limit the coverage provided under Covered Risk 11, 16, 17, 18, 19, 20, 21, 22, 23, 24, 27 or 28); or

   (e) resulting in loss or damage that would not have been sustained if the Insured Claimant had paid value for the Insured Mortgage.

4. Unenforceability of the lien of the Insured Mortgage because of the inability or failure of an Insured to comply with applicable doing-business laws of the state where the Land is situated.

5. Invalidity or unenforceability in whole or in part of the lien of the Insured Mortgage that arises out of the transaction evidenced by the Insured Mortgage and is based upon usury, or any consumer credit protection or truth-in-lending law. This Exclusion does not modify or limit the coverage provided in Covered Risk 26.

6. Any claim of invalidity, unenforceability or lack of priority of the lien of the Insured Mortgage as to Advances or modifications made after the Insured has Knowledge that the vestee shown in Schedule A is no longer the owner of the estate or interest covered by this policy. This Exclusion does not modify or limit the coverage provided in Covered Risk 11.

7. Any lien on the Title for real estate taxes or assessments imposed by governmental authority and created or attaching subsequent to Date of Policy. This Exclusion does not modify or limit the coverage provided in Covered Risk 11(b) or 25.

8. The failure of the residential structure, or any portion of it, to have been constructed before, on or after Date of Policy in accordance with applicable building codes. This Exclusion does not modify or limit the coverage provided in Covered Risk 5 or 6.

Appendix Figure 3 | ALTA Loan Policy (continued)

American Land Title Association	Expanded Coverage Residential Loan Policy
	Revised 1/01/08

EXPANDED COVERAGE RESIDENTIAL LOAN POLICY
FOR A ONE-TO-FOUR FAMILY RESIDENCE

Issued By

BLANK TITLE INSURANCE COMPANY

SCHEDULE A

Name and Address of Title Insurance Company:

[File No.:] Policy　　　　　　　　No.:

Loan No.:

Street Address of the Land:

Policy Amount: $　　　　　　　[Premium: $　　　　　　　　]

Date of Policy:　　　　　　　　[at a.m./p.m.]

1. Name of Insured:
2. The estate or interest in the Land that is encumbered by the Insured Mortgage is:
3. Title is vested in:
4. The Insured Mortgage and its assignments, if any, are described as follows:
5. The Land referred to in this policy is described as follows:

Appendix Figure 3 | ALTA Loan Policy (continued)

American Land Title Association Expanded Coverage Residential Loan Policy
Revised 1/01/08

EXPANDED COVERAGE RESIDENTIAL LOAN POLICY
FOR A ONE-TO-FOUR FAMILY RESIDENCE

Issued By

BLANK TITLE INSURANCE COMPANY

SCHEDULE B - PART I

[File No.:] Policy No.:

EXCEPTIONS FROM COVERAGE

This policy does not insure against loss or damage (and the Company will not pay costs, attorneys' fees or expenses) that arise by reason of:

[1. The following state statutes, reference to which are made part of the ALTA 8.1-06 Environmental Protection Lien Endorsement incorporated into this Policy:]

SCHEDULE B - PART II

In addition to the matters set forth in Part I of this Schedule, the Title is subject to the following matters, and the Company insures against loss or damage sustained in the event that they are not subordinate to the lien of the Insured Mortgage:

Appendix Figure 3 | ALTA Loan Policy (continued)

American Land Title Association

Expanded Coverage Residential Loan Policy

Revised 1/01/08

CONDITIONS

1. DEFINITION OF TERMS

   The following terms when used in this policy mean:

   (a) Advances": Disbursements of Indebtedness made after the Date of Policy as provided by the Insured Mortgage.

   (b) "Amount of Insurance": One hundred twenty-five percent (125%) of the Policy Amount stated in Schedule A, as may be increased or decreased by endorsement to this policy, increased by Section 8(b) or decreased by Section 10 of these Conditions.

   (c) "Date of Policy": The date designated as "Date of Policy" in Schedule A.

   (d) "Entity": A corporation, partnership, trust, limited liability company, or other similar legal entity.

   (e) "Indebtedness": The obligation secured by the Insured Mortgage including one evidenced by electronic means authorized by law, and if that obligation is the payment of a debt, the Indebtedness is the sum of

   (i) the amount of the principal disbursed as of Date of Policy;

   (ii) the amount of the principal disbursed subsequent to Date of Policy;

   (iii) the construction loan advances made subsequent to Date of Policy for the purpose of financing in whole or in part the construction of an improvement to the Land or related to the Land that the Insured was and continued to be obligated to advance at Date of Policy and at the date of the Advance;

   (iv) interest on the loan;

   (v) the prepayment premiums, exit fees, and other similar fees or penalties allowed by law;

   (vi) the expenses of foreclosure and any other costs of enforcement;

   (vii) the amounts advanced to assure compliance with laws or to protect the lien or the priority of the lien of the Insured Mortgage before the acquisition of the estate or interest in the Title;

   (viii) the amounts to pay taxes and insurance; and

   (ix) the reasonable amounts expended to prevent deterioration of improvements;

   but the Indebtedness is reduced by the total of all payments and by any amount forgiven by an Insured.

   (f) "Insured": The Insured named in Schedule A.

   (i) The term "Insured" also includes

   (A) the owner of the Indebtedness and each successor in ownership of the Indebtedness, whether the owner or successor owns the Indebtedness for its own account or as a trustee or other fiduciary, except a successor who is an obligor under the provisions of Section 12(c) of these Conditions;

   (B) the person or Entity who has "control" of the "transferable record," if the Indebtedness is evidenced by a "transferable record," as these terms are defined by applicable electronic transactions law;

   (C) successors to an Insured by dissolution, merger, consolidation, distribution, or reorganization;

   (D) successors to an Insured by its conversion to another kind of Entity;

   (E) a grantee of an Insured under a deed delivered without payment of actual valuable consideration conveying the Title

   (1) if the stock, shares, memberships, or other equity interests of the grantee are wholly-owned by the named Insured,

Appendix Figure 3 | ALTA Loan Policy (continued)

American Land Title AssociationExpanded Coverage Residential Loan Policy

Revised 1/01/08

(2) if the grantee wholly owns the named Insured, or

(3) if the grantee is wholly-owned by an affiliated Entity of the named Insured, provided the affiliated Entity and the named Insured are both wholly-owned by the same person or Entity;

(F) any government agency or instrumentality that is an insurer or guarantor under an insurance contract or guaranty insuring or guaranteeing the Indebtedness secured by the Insured Mortgage, or any part of it, whether named as an Insured or not;

(ii) With regard to (A), (B), (C), (D) , and (E) reserving, however, all rights and defenses as to any successor that the Company would have had against any predecessor Insured, unless the successor acquired the Indebtedness as a purchaser for value without Knowledge of the asserted defect, lien, encumbrance, or other matter insured against by this policy.

(g) "Insured Claimant": An Insured claiming loss or damage.

(h) "Insured Mortgage": The Mortgage described in paragraph 4 of Schedule A.

(i) "Knowledge" or "Known": Actual knowledge, not constructive knowledge or notice that may be imputed to an Insured by reason of the Public Records or any other records that impart constructive notice of matters affecting the Title.

(j) "Land": The land described in Schedule A, and affixed improvements that by law constitute real property. The term "Land" does not include any property beyond the lines of the area described in Schedule A, nor any right, title, interest, estate, or easement in abutting streets, roads, avenues, alleys, lanes, ways, or waterways, but this does not modify or limit the extent that a right of access to and from the Land is insured by this policy.

(k) "Mortgage": Mortgage, deed of trust, trust deed, or other security instrument, including one evidenced by electronic means authorized by law.

(l) "Public Records": Records established under state statutes at Date of Policy for the purpose of imparting constructive notice of matters relating to real property to purchasers for value and without Knowledge. With respect to Covered Risk 5(d), "Public Records" shall also include environmental protection liens filed in the records of the clerk of the United States District Court for the district where the Land is located.

(m) "Title": The estate or interest described in Schedule A.

(n) "Unmarketable Title": Title affected by an alleged or apparent matter that would permit a prospective purchaser or lessee of the Title or lender on the Title or a prospective purchaser of the Insured Mortgage to be released from the obligation to purchase, lease, or lend if there is a contractual condition requiring the delivery of marketable title.

2. CONTINUATION OF INSURANCE

The coverage of this policy shall continue in force as of Date of Policy in favor of an Insured after acquisition of the Title by an Insured or after conveyance by an Insured, but only so long as the Insured retains an estate or interest in the Land, or holds an obligation secured by a purchase money Mortgage given by a purchaser from the Insured, or only so long as the Insured shall have liability by reason of warranties in any transfer or conveyance of the Title. This policy shall not continue in force in favor of any purchaser from the Insured of either (i) an estate or interest in the Land, or (ii) an obligation secured by a purchase money Mortgage given to the Insured.

3. NOTICE OF CLAIM TO BE GIVEN BY INSURED CLAIMANT

The Insured shall notify the Company promptly in writing (i) in case of any litigation as set forth in Section 5(a) of these Conditions, (ii) in case Knowledge shall come to an Insured of any claim of title or interest that is adverse to the Title or the lien of the Insured Mortgage, as insured, and that might cause loss or damage for which the Company may be liable by virtue of this policy, or (iii) if the Title or the lien of the Insured Mortgage, as insured, is rejected as Unmarketable Title. If the Company is prejudiced by the failure of the Insured Claimant to provide prompt notice, the Company's liability to the Insured Claimant under the policy shall be reduced to the extent of the prejudice.

Appendix Figure 3 | ALTA Loan Policy (continued)

American Land Title Association	Expanded Coverage Residential Loan Policy
	Revised 1/01/08

4. PROOF OF LOSS

In the event the Company is unable to determine the amount of loss or damage, the Company may, at its option, require as a condition of payment that the Insured Claimant furnish a signed proof of loss. The proof of loss must describe the defect, lien, encumbrance, or other matter insured against by this policy that constitutes the basis of loss or damage and shall state, to the extent possible, the basis of calculating the amount of the loss or damage.

5. DEFENSE AND PROSECUTION OF ACTIONS

(a) Upon written request by the Insured, and subject to the options contained in Section 7 of these Conditions, the Company, at its own cost and without unreasonable delay, shall provide for the defense of an Insured in litigation in which any third party asserts a claim covered by this policy adverse to the Insured. This obligation is limited to only those stated causes of action alleging matters insured against by this policy. The Company shall have the right to select counsel of its choice (subject to the right of the Insured to object for reasonable cause) to represent the Insured as to those stated causes of action. It shall not be liable for and will not pay the fees of any other counsel. The Company will not pay any fees, costs, or expenses incurred by the Insured in the defense of those causes of action that allege matters not insured against by this policy.

(b) The Company shall have the right, in addition to the options contained in Section 7 of these Conditions, at its own cost, to institute and prosecute any action or proceeding or to do any other act that in its opinion may be necessary or desirable to establish the Title or the lien of the Insured Mortgage, as insured, or to prevent or reduce loss or damage to the Insured. The Company may take any appropriate action under the terms of this policy, whether or not it shall be liable to the Insured. The exercise of these rights shall not be an admission of liability or waiver of any provision of this policy. If the Company exercises its rights under this subsection, it must do so diligently.

(c) Whenever the Company brings an action or asserts a defense as required or permitted by this policy, the Company may pursue the litigation to a final determination by a court of competent jurisdiction, and it expressly reserves the right, in its sole discretion, to appeal any adverse judgment or order.

6. DUTY OF INSURED CLAIMANT TO COOPERATE

(a) In all cases where this policy permits or requires the Company to prosecute or provide for the defense of any action or proceeding and any appeals, the Insured shall secure to the Company the right to so prosecute or provide defense in the action or proceeding, including the right to use, at its option, the name of the Insured for this purpose. Whenever requested by the Company, the Insured, at the Company's expense, shall give the Company all reasonable aid (i) in securing evidence, obtaining witnesses, prosecuting or defending the action or proceeding, or effecting settlement, and (ii) in any other lawful act that in the opinion of the Company may be necessary or desirable to establish the Title, the lien of the Insured Mortgage, or any other matter as insured. If the Company is prejudiced by the failure of the Insured to furnish the required cooperation, the Company's obligations to the Insured under the policy shall terminate, including any liability or obligation to defend, prosecute, or continue any litigation, with regard to the matter or matters requiring such cooperation.

(b) The Company may reasonably require the Insured Claimant to submit to examination under oath by any authorized representative of the Company and to produce for examination, inspection, and copying, at such reasonable times and places as may be designated by the authorized representative of the Company, all records, in whatever medium maintained, including books, ledgers, checks, memoranda, correspondence, reports, e-mails, disks, tapes, and videos whether bearing a date before or after Date of Policy, that reasonably pertain to the loss or damage. Further, if requested by any authorized representative of the Company, the Insured Claimant shall grant its permission, in writing, for any authorized representative of the Company to examine, inspect, and copy all of these records in the custody or control of a third party that reasonably pertain to the loss or damage. All information designated as confidential by the Insured Claimant provided to the Company pursuant to this Section shall not be disclosed to others unless, in the reasonable judgment of the Company, it is necessary in the administration of the claim. Failure of the Insured Claimant to submit for examination under oath, produce any reasonably requested information, or grant permission to secure reasonably necessary information from third parties as required in this subsection, unless prohibited by law or governmental regulation, shall terminate any liability of the Company under this policy as to that claim.

Appendix Figure 3 | ALTA Loan Policy (continued)

American Land Title Association	Expanded Coverage Residential Loan Policy
	Revised 1/01/08

7. OPTIONS TO PAY OR OTHERWISE SETTLE CLAIMS; TERMINATION OF LIABILITY

In case of a claim under this policy, the Company shall have the following additional options:

(a) To Pay or Tender Payment of the Amount of Insurance or to Purchase the Indebtedness.

   (i) To pay or tender payment of the Amount of Insurance under this policy together with any costs, attorneys' fees, and expenses incurred by the Insured Claimant that were authorized by the Company up to the time of payment or tender of payment and that the Company is obligated to pay; or

   (ii) To purchase the Indebtedness for the amount of the Indebtedness on the date of purchase, together with any costs, attorneys' fees, and expenses incurred by the Insured Claimant that were authorized by the Company up to the time of purchase and that the Company is obligated to pay.

   When the Company purchases the Indebtedness, the Insured shall transfer, assign, and convey to the Company the Indebtedness and the Insured Mortgage, together with any collateral security.

   Upon the exercise by the Company of either of the options provided for in subsections (a)(i) or (ii), all liability and obligations of the Company to the Insured under this policy, other than to make the payment required in those subsections, shall terminate, including any liability or obligation to defend, prosecute, or continue any litigation.

(b) To Pay or Otherwise Settle With Parties Other Than the Insured or With the Insured Claimant.

   (i) to pay or otherwise settle with other parties for or in the name of an Insured Claimant any claim insured against under this policy. In addition, the Company will pay any costs, attorneys' fees, and expenses incurred by the Insured Claimant that were authorized by the Company up to the time of payment and that the Company is obligated to pay; or

   (ii) to pay or otherwise settle with the Insured Claimant the loss or damage provided for under this policy, together with any costs, attorneys' fees, and expenses incurred by the Insured Claimant that were authorized by the Company up to the time of payment and that the Company is obligated to pay.

   Upon the exercise by the Company of either of the options provided for in subsections (b)(i) or (ii), the Company's obligations to the Insured under this policy for the claimed loss or damage, other than the payments required to be made, shall terminate, including any liability or obligation to defend, prosecute, or continue any litigation.

8. DETERMINATION AND EXTENT OF LIABILITY

This policy is a contract of indemnity against actual monetary loss or damage sustained or incurred by the Insured Claimant who has suffered loss or damage by reason of matters insured against by this policy.

(a) The extent of liability of the Company for loss or damage under this policy shall not exceed the least of

   (i) The Amount of Insurance,

   (ii) the Indebtedness,

   (iii) the difference between the value of the Title as insured and the value of the Title subject to the risk insured against by this policy, provided, however, that this Section 8(a)(iii) shall not apply when the defect, lien, encumbrance or other matter insured against by this policy results in a total failure of the lien of the Insured Mortgage to attach to the Title, or

   (iv) if a government agency or instrumentality is the Insured Claimant, the amount it paid in the acquisition of the Title or the Insured Mortgage in satisfaction of its insurance contract or guaranty.

(b) If the Company pursues its rights under Section 5 of these Conditions and is unsuccessful in establishing the Title or the lien of the Insured Mortgage, as insured,

Appendix Figure 3 | ALTA Loan Policy (continued)

American Land Title Association
Expanded Coverage Residential Loan Policy
Revised 1/01/08

    (i) the Amount of Insurance shall be increased by 10%, and

    (ii) the Insured Claimant shall have the right to have the loss or damage determined either as of the date the claim was made by the Insured Claimant or as of the date it is settled and paid.

 (c) In the event the Insured has acquired the Title in the manner described in Section 2 of these Conditions or has conveyed the Title, then the extent of liability of the Company shall continue as set forth in Section 8(a) of these Conditions.

 (d) In addition to the extent of liability under (a), (b), and (c), the Company will also pay those costs, attorneys' fees, and expenses incurred in accordance with Sections 5 and 7 of these Conditions.

9. LIMITATION OF LIABILITY

 (a) If the Company establishes the Title, or removes the alleged defect, lien, or encumbrance, or cures the lack of a right of access to or from the Land, or cures the claim of Unmarketable Title, or establishes the lien of the Insured Mortgage, all as insured, in a reasonably diligent manner by any method, including litigation and the completion of any appeals, it shall have fully performed its obligations with respect to that matter and shall not be liable for any loss or damage caused to the Insured.

 (b) n the event of any litigation, including litigation by the Company or with the Company's consent, the Company shall have no liability for loss or damage until there has been a final determination by a court of competent jurisdiction, and disposition of all appeals, adverse to the Title or to the lien of the Insured Mortgage, as insured.

 (c) The Company shall not be liable for loss or damage to the Insured for liability voluntarily assumed by the Insured in settling any claim or suit without the prior written consent of the Company.

10. REDUCTION OF INSURANCE; REDUCTION OR TERMINATION OF LIABILITY

 (a) All payments under this policy, except payments made for costs, attorneys' fees, and expenses, shall reduce the Amount of Insurance by the amount of the payment. However, any payments made prior to the acquisition of Title as provided in Section 2 of these Conditions shall not reduce the Amount of Insurance afforded under this policy except to the extent that the payments reduce the Indebtedness.

 (b) The voluntary satisfaction or release of the Insured Mortgage shall terminate all liability of the Company except as provided in Section 2 of these Conditions.

11. PAYMENT OF LOSS

When liability and the extent of loss or damage have been definitely fixed in accordance with these Conditions, the payment shall be made within 30 days.

12. RIGHTS OF RECOVERY UPON PAYMENT OR SETTLEMENT

 (a) The Company's Right to Recover

Whenever the Company shall have settled and paid a claim under this policy, it shall be subrogated and entitled to the rights of the Insured Claimant in the Title or Insured Mortgage and all other rights and remedies in respect to the claim that the Insured Claimant has against any person or property, to the extent of the amount of any loss, costs, attorneys' fees, and expenses paid by the Company. If requested by the Company, the Insured Claimant shall execute documents to evidence the transfer to the Company of these rights and remedies. The Insured Claimant shall permit the Company to sue, compromise, or settle in the name of the Insured Claimant and to use the name of the Insured Claimant in any transaction or litigation involving these rights and remedies.

If a payment on account of a claim does not fully cover the loss of the Insured Claimant, the Company shall defer the exercise of its right to recover until after the Insured Claimant shall have recovered its loss.

Appendix Figure 3 | ALTA Loan Policy (continued)

American Land Title Association	Expanded Coverage Residential Loan Policy
	Revised 1/01/08

    (b) The Insured's Rights and Limitations

        (i) The owner of the Indebtedness may release or substitute the personal liability of any debtor or guarantor, extend or otherwise modify the terms of payment, release a portion of the Title from the lien of the Insured Mortgage, or release any collateral security for the Indebtedness, if it does not affect the enforceability or priority of the lien of the Insured Mortgage.

        (ii) If the Insured exercises a right provided in (b)(i), but has Knowledge of any claim adverse to the Title or the lien of the Insured Mortgage insured against by this policy, the Company shall be required to pay only that part of any losses insured against by this policy that shall exceed the amount, if any, lost to the Company by reason of the impairment by the Insured Claimant of the Company's right of subrogation.

    (c) The Company's Rights Against Noninsured Obligors

    The Company's right of subrogation includes the Insured's rights against non-insured obligors including the rights of the Insured to indemnities, guarantees, other policies of insurance, or bonds, notwithstanding any terms or conditions contained in those instruments that address subrogation rights.

    The Company's right of subrogation shall not be avoided by acquisition of the Insured Mortgage by an obligor (except an obligor described in Section 1(f)(i)(F) of these Conditions) who acquires the Insured Mortgage as a result of an indemnity, guarantee, other policy of insurance, or bond, and the obligor will not be an Insured under this policy.

13. ARBITRATION

Either the Company or the Insured may demand that the claim or controversy shall be submitted to arbitration pursuant to the Title Insurance Arbitration Rules of the American Land Title Association ("Rules"). Except as provided in the Rules, there shall be no joinder or consolidation with claims or controversies of other persons. Arbitrable matters may include, but are not limited to, any controversy or claim between the Company and the Insured arising out of or relating to this policy, any service in connection with its issuance or the breach of a policy provision, or to any other controversy or claim arising out of the transaction giving rise to this policy. All arbitrable matters when the Amount of Insurance is $2,000,000 or less shall be arbitrated at the option of either the Company or the Insured. All arbitrable matters when the Amount of Insurance is in excess of $2,000,000 shall be arbitrated only when agreed to by both the Company and the Insured. Arbitration pursuant to this policy and under the Rules shall be binding upon the parties. Judgment upon the award rendered by the Arbitrator(s) may be entered in any court of competent jurisdiction.

14. LIABILITY LIMITED TO THIS POLICY; POLICY ENTIRE CONTRACT

    (a) This policy together with all endorsements, if any, attached to it by the Company is the entire policy and contract between the Insured and the Company. In interpreting any provision of this policy, this policy shall be construed as a whole.

    (b) Any claim of loss or damage that arises out of the status of the Title or lien of the Insured Mortgage or by any action asserting such claim shall be restricted to this policy.

    (c) Any amendment of or endorsement to this policy must be in writing and authenticated by an authorized person, or expressly incorporated by Schedule A of this policy.

    (d) Each endorsement to this policy issued at any time is made a part of this policy and is subject to all of its terms and provisions. Except as the endorsement expressly states, it does not (i) modify any of the terms and provisions of the policy, (ii) modify any prior endorsement, (iii) extend the Date of Policy, or (iv) increase the Amount of Insurance.

15. SEVERABILITY

In the event any provision of this policy, in whole or in part, is held invalid or unenforceable under applicable law, the policy shall be deemed not to include that provision or such part held to be invalid, but all other provisions shall remain in full force and effect.

Appendix Figure 3 | ALTA Loan Policy (continued)

American Land Title Association — Expanded Coverage Residential Loan Policy
Revised 1/01/08

16. CHOICE OF LAW; FORUM

(a) Choice of Law: The Insured acknowledges the Company has underwritten the risks covered by this policy and determined the premium charged therefor in reliance upon the law affecting interests in real property and applicable to the interpretation, rights, remedies, or enforcement of policies of title insurance of the jurisdiction where the Land is located.

Therefore, the court or an arbitrator shall apply the law of the jurisdiction where the Land is located to determine the validity of claims against the Title or the lien of the Insured Mortgage that are adverse to the Insured and to interpret and enforce the terms of this policy. In neither case shall the court or arbitrator apply its conflicts of law principles to determine the applicable law.

(b) (b) Choice of Forum: Any litigation or other proceeding brought by the Insured against the Company must be filed only in a state or federal court within the United States of America or its territories having appropriate jurisdiction.

17. NOTICES, WHERE SENT

Any notice of claim and any other notice or statement in writing required to be given to the Company under this policy must be given to the Company at [fill in].

NOTE: Bracketed [ ] material optional

Appendix Figure 4 | ALTA Endorsement Forms List

Endorsement	Name	Current
ALTA Endorsement Form 1	06 Street Assessments	(06-17-06)
ALTA Endorsement Form 2	06 Truth in Lending	(06-17-06)
ALTA Endorsement Form 3	06 Zoning Unimproved Land	(06-17-06)
ALTA Endorsement Form 3.1	06 Zoning - Completed Structure	(06-17-06)
ALTA Endorsement Form 4	06 Condominium	(06-17-06)
ALTA Endorsement Form 4.1	06 Condominium	(06-17-06)
ALTA Endorsement Form 5	06 Planned Unit Development	(06-17-06)
ALTA Endorsement Form 5.1	06 Planned Unit Development	(06-17-06)
ALTA Endorsement Form 6	06 Variable Rate Mortgage	(06-17-06)
ALTA Endorsement Form 6.2	06 Variable Rate Mortgage - Negative Amortization	(06-17-06)
ALTA Endorsement Form 7	06 Manufactured Housing Unit	(06-17-06)
ALTA Endorsement Form 7.1	06 Manufactured Housing - Conversion; Loan	(06-17-06)
ALTA Endorsement Form 7.2	06 Manufactured Housing - Conversion: Owner's	(06-17-06)
ALTA Endorsement Form 8.1	06 Environmental Protection	(06-17-06)
ALTA Endorsement Form 9	06 Restrictions, Encroachments, Minerals	(06-17-06)
ALTA Endorsement Form 9.1	06 Restrictions, Encroachments, Minerals Owner's Policy: Unimproved Land	(06-17-06)
ALTA Endorsement Form 9.2	06 Restrictions, Encroachments, and Minerals - Owner's Policy: Improved Land	(06-17-06)
ALTA Endorsement Form 9.3	06 Restrictions, Encroachments, Minerals - Loan Policy	(06-17-06)
ALTA Endorsement Form 9.4	06 Restrictions, Encroachments, Minerals - Owner's Policy: Unimproved Land	(06-17-06)
ALTA Endorsement Form 9.5	06 Restrictions, Encroachments, Minerals - Owner's Policy: Improved Land	(06-17-06)
ALTA Endorsement Form 10	06 Assignment	(06-17-06)
ALTA Endorsement Form 10.1	06 Assignment and Date Down	(06-17-06)
ALTA Endorsement Form 11	06 Mortgage Modification	(06-17-06)
ALTA Endorsement Form 12	06 Aggregation	(06-17-06)
ALTA Endorsement Form 13	06 Leasehold - Owners	(06-17-06)
ALTA Endorsement Form 13.1	06 Leasehold - Loan	(06-17-06)
ALTA Endorsement Form 14	06 Future Advance - Priority	(06-17-06)
ALTA Endorsement Form 14.1	06 Future Advance - Knowledge	(06-17-06)
ALTA Endorsement Form 14.2	06 Future Advance - Letter of Credit	(06-17-06)
ALTA Endorsement Form 14.3	06 Future Advance - Reverse Mortgage	(06-17-06)
ALTA Endorsement Form 15	06 Non-Imputation - Full Equity Transfer	(06-17-06)
ALTA Endorsement Form 15.1	06 Non-Imputation - Additional Insured	(06-17-06)
ALTA Endorsement Form 15.2	06 Non-Imputation - Partial Equity Transfer	(06-17-06)
ALTA Endorsement Form 16	06 Mezzanine Financing	(06-17-06)
ALTA Endorsement Form 17	06 Access and Entry	(06-17-06)
ALTA Endorsement Form 17.1	06 Indirect Access and Entry	(06-17-06)
ALTA Endorsement Form 18	06 Single Tax Parcel	(06-17-06)
ALTA Endorsement Form 18.1	06 Multiple Tax Parcel	(06-17-06)
ALTA Endorsement Form 19	06 Contiguity-Multiple Parcels	(06-17-06)
ALTA Endorsement Form 19.1	06 Contiguity-Single Parcel	(06-17-06)
ALTA Endorsement Form 20	06 First Loss-Multiple Parcel Transactions	(06-17-06)
ALTA Endorsement Form 21	06 Creditors' Rights	(06-17-06)
ALTA Endorsement Form 22	06 Location	(06-17-06)
ALTA Endorsement Form 22.1	06 Location and Map	(06-17-06)
ALTA Endorsement Form JR1	Supplemental Coverage	(10-19-96)
ALTA Endorsement Form JR2	Revolving Credit/Variable Rate	(10-19-96)

Appendix Figure 5 | ALTA Closing Protection Letter and Explanation

American Land Title Association	Expanded Coverage Residential Loan Policy
	Revised 1/01/08

ALTA CLOSING PROTECTION LETTER
BLANK TITLE INSURANCE COMPANY

Name and Address of Addressee:

Date:

Name of Issuing Agent or Approved Attorney (hereafter, "Issuing Agent" or "Approved Attorney", as the case may require):

[Identity of settlement agent and status as either Issuing Agent or Approved Attorney appears here.]

Re: Closing Protection Letter

Dear

Blank Title Insurance Company (the "Company") agrees, subject to the Conditions and Exclusions set forth below, to reimburse you for actual loss incurred by you in connection with closings of real estate transactions conducted by the Issuing Agent or Approved Attorney, provided:

(A) title insurance of the Company is specified for your protection in connection with the closing; and

(B) you are to be the (i) lender secured by a mortgage (including any other security instrument) of an interest in land, its assignees or a warehouse lender, (ii) purchaser of an interest in land, or (iii) lessee of an interest in land

and provided the loss arises out of:

1. Failure of the Issuing Agent or Approved Attorney to comply with your written closing instructions to the extent that they relate to (a) the status of the title to that interest in land or the validity, enforceability and priority of the lien of the mortgage on that interest in land, including the obtaining of documents and the disbursement of funds necessary to establish the status of title or lien, or (b) the obtaining of any other document, specifically required by you, but only to the extent the failure to obtain the other document affects the status of the title to that interest in land or the validity, enforceability and priority of the lien of the mortgage on that interest in land, and not to the extent that your instructions require a determination of the validity, enforceability or the effectiveness of the other document, or

2. Fraud, dishonesty or negligence of the Issuing Agent or Approved Attorney in handling your funds or documents in connection with the closings to the extent that fraud, dishonesty or negligence relates to the status of the title to that interest in land or to the validity, enforceability, and priority of the lien of the mortgage on that interest in land.

If you are a lender protected under the foregoing paragraph, your borrower, your assignee and your warehouse lender in connection with a loan secured by a mortgage shall be protected as if this letter were addressed to them.

<u>Conditions and Exclusions</u>

1. The Company will not be liable to you for loss arising out of:

   A. Failure of the Issuing Agent or Approved Attorney to comply with your closing instructions which require title insurance protection inconsistent with that set forth in the title insurance binder or commitment issued by the Company. Instructions which require the removal of specific exceptions to title or compliance with the requirements contained in the binder or commitment shall not be deemed to be inconsistent.

   B. Loss or impairment of your funds in the course of collection or while on deposit with a bank due to bank failure, insolvency or suspension, except as shall result from failure of the Issuing Agent or the Approved Attorney to comply with your written closing instructions to deposit the funds in a bank which you designated by name.

Appendix Figure 5 | ALTA Closing Protection Letter and Explanation (continued)

    C.   Defects, liens, encumbrances or other matters in connection with your purchase, lease or loan transactions except to the extent that protection against those defects, liens, encumbrances or other matters is afforded by a policy of title insurance not inconsistent with your closing instructions.

    D.   Fraud, dishonesty or negligence of your employee, agent, attorney or broker.

    E.   Your settlement or release of any claim without the written consent of the Company.

    F.   Any matters created, suffered, assumed or agreed to by you or known to you.

2. If the closing is to be conducted by an Approved Attorney, a title insurance binder or commitment for the issuance of a policy of title insurance of the Company must have been received by you prior to the transmission of your final closing instructions to the Approved Attorney.

3. When the Company shall have reimbursed you pursuant to this letter, it shall be subrogated to all rights and remedies which you would have had against any person or property had you not been so reimbursed. Liability of the Company for reimbursement shall be reduced to the extent that you have knowingly and voluntarily impaired the value of this right of subrogation.

4. The Issuing Agent is the Company's agent only for the limited purpose of issuing title insurance policies. Neither the Issuing Agent nor the Approved Attorney is the Company's agent for the purpose of providing other closing or settlement services. The Company's liability for your losses arising from those other closing or settlement services is strictly limited to the protection expressly provided in this letter. Any liability of the Company for loss does not include liability for loss resulting from the negligence, fraud or bad faith of any party to a real estate transaction other than an Issuing Agent or Approved Attorney, the lack of creditworthiness of any borrower connected with a real estate transaction, or the failure of any collateral to adequately secure a loan connected with a real estate transaction. However, this letter does not affect the Company's liability with respect to its title insurance binders, commitments or policies.

5. Either the Company or you may demand that any claim arising under this letter be submitted to arbitration pursuant to the Title Insurance Arbitration Rules of the American Land Title Association, unless you have a policy of title insurance for the applicable transaction with an Amount of Insurance greater than $2,000,000. If you have a policy of title insurance for the applicable transaction with an Amount of Insurance greater than $2,000,000, a claim arising under this letter may be submitted to arbitration only when agreed to by both the Company and you.

6. You must promptly send written notice of a claim under this letter to the Company at its principal office at _____ _____. The Company is not liable for a loss if the written notice is not received within one year from the date of the closing.

7. The protection herein offered extends only to real property transactions in [State].

Any previous closing protection letter or similar agreement is hereby cancelled, except for closings of your real estate transactions for which you have previously sent (or within 30 days hereafter send) written closing instructions to the Issuing Agent or Approved Attorney.

BLANK TITLE INSURANCE COMPANY

By: _____

(The name of a particular issuing agent or approved attorney may be inserted in lieu of reference to Issuing Agent or Approved Attorney contained in this letter and the words "Underwritten Title Company" may be inserted in lieu of Issuing Agent.)

Appendix Figure 6 | Property Sketch or Plat

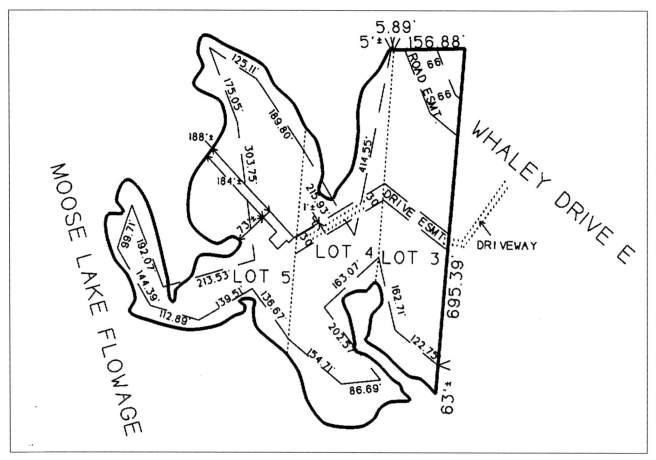

Source: Access Information Systems, Inc., Bloomington, MN.

Appendix Figure 7 | Sample Inspection

Access Information Systems, Inc.
Property Inspection Report

Order Number: _____

Address On Building: _____

Character Of Improvements?
- (✓) 1 Sty   ( ) Frame   (✓) Residential
- ( ) 1 1/2 Sty ( ) Brick   ( ) Townhouse
- ( ) 2 Sty   ( ) Stucco   ( ) Condo
- ( ) Other   (✓) Other   ( ) Other _____
                 Log

Garage?   **Any Alley?**
- ( ) Attached   ( ) Yes
- ( ) Not Attached   (✓) No
- (✓) None
- ____ Car

Estimated Age of Improvements?
- ( ) New Construction
- ( ) Less than 1 year
- (✓) 1 to 5 years
- ( ) 5 to 15 years
- ( ) 15 years or older

Any Apparent Recent Improvements?
- (✓) Yes   Describe: *Dumpster sitting on Lot 4*
- ( ) No   *Lumber delivered*

Apparent Easements?
- (✓) Yes   Describe: *Access Easement over*
- ( ) No   *land to east*

Are There Any Fences On Property?
- ( ) Yes   Describe: _____
- (✓) No

Inspection Date: _____

Do Improvements On Adjoining Property Appear To Encroach?
- ( ) Yes   Describe: _____
- (✓) No

Any Party Walls?
- ( ) Yes   Where: _____
- (✓) No

Do Improvements Appear To Be Within Property Lines?
- ( ) No   Describe: _____
- (✓) Yes

Access to Property?
- ( ) Street / Alley
- ( ) Shared Drive
- (✓) Access Esmt
- ( ) Other _____

Persons In Possession?
- (✓) Occupied (no response)
- ( ) Unoccupied
- ( ) Owner
- ( ) Workmen
- ( ) Other _____

Other Information:
_____
_____
_____

Inspected By: _____

Plat drawing prepared by:
ACCESS INFORMATION SYSTEMS, INC, 1210A W 96TH ST, BLOOMINGTON, MN 55431
PHONE NUMBER (952) 888-8503, FAX NUMBER (952) 888-4576

Appendix Figure 8 | Affidavit of Buyer

(Top 3 inches reserved for recording data)

AFFIDAVIT REGARDING PURCHASER
by Individual(s)

Minnesota Uniform Conveyancing Blanks
Form 50.1.1 (2006)

State of Minnesota, County of _____

_____ being first duly sworn on oath say(s) that:
(insert name of each affiant)

1. (They are) (____ he is) (____ he knows) _____ the person(s) named as _____ in the document dated _____ and filed for record _____ as Document Number _____
   (month/day/year) *(month/day/year)*
   (or in Book _____ of _____, Page _____), in the Office of the ☐ County Recorder ☐ Registrar of Titles
   (check the applicable boxes)
   of _____ County, Minnesota.

2. Said person(s) (is) (are) of legal age and under no legal disability with place of business(es) respectively at _____

and for the last ten (10) years (has)(have) resided at:

3. There are no:
   a. Bankruptcy, divorce or dissolution proceedings involving said person(s) during the time period in which said person(s) have had any interest in the premises described in the above document ("**Premises**");
   b. Unsatisfied judgments of record against said person(s) nor, to your Affiant(s) knowledge, any actions pending in any courts which affect the Premises;
   c. Tax liens filed against said person(s);
except as herein stated:

Page 1 of 2

Appendix Figure 8 | Affidavit of Buyer (continued)

Page 2 of 2 Minnesota Uniform Conveyancing Blanks **Form 50.1.1**

4. Any bankruptcy, divorce or dissolution proceeding of record against parties with the same or similar names, during the time period in which the above-named person(s) (has) (have) had any interest in the Premises, are not against the above-named person(s).

5. Any judgments or tax liens of record against parties with the same or similar names are not against the above-named person(s).

6. Said person(s) (has) (have) not ordered or arranged for any labor or materials to be furnished to the Premises for which payment has not been made.

7. There are no persons in possession of any portion of the Premises of which Affiant(s) (has) (have) knowledge, other than pursuant to a recorded document, except as stated herein:

Affiant(s) know(s) the matters herein stated are true and make(s) this Affidavit for the purpose of inducing the acceptance of title to the Premises.

Affiant

_____
(signature)

_____
(signature)

Signed and sworn to before me on _____, by _____
                                  (month/day/year)
_____
                        (insert name of person making statement)

(Seal, if any)

_____
(signature of notarial officer)
Title (and Rank): _____
My commission expires: _____
                            (month/day/year)

THIS INSTRUMENT WAS DRAFTED BY:
(insert name and address)

Appendix Figure 9 | Affidavit of Seller

(Top 3 inches reserved for recording data)

AFFIDAVIT REGARDING SELLER
by Individual(s)

Minnesota Uniform Conveyancing Blanks
Form 50.1.2 (2006)

State of Minnesota, County of _____

_____ being first duly sworn on oath say(s) that:
(insert name of each affiant)

1. (They are) (____ he is) (____ he knows) _____ the person(s) named as _____ in the document dated _____ and filed for record _____ as Document Number _____
(month/day/year) (month/day/year)
(or in Book _____ of _____, Page _____), in the Office of the ☐ County Recorder ☐ Registrar of Titles
(check the applicable boxes)
of _____ County, Minnesota.

2. Said person(s) (is) (are) of legal age and under no legal disability with place of business(es) respectively at _____
_____
and for the last ten (10) years (has)(have) resided at:

3. There are no:
   a. Bankruptcy, divorce or dissolution proceedings involving said person(s) during the time period in which said person(s) have had any interest in the premises described in the above document ("**Premises**");
   b. Unsatisfied judgments of record against said person(s) nor, to your Affiant(s) knowledge, any actions pending in any courts which affect the Premises;
   c. Tax liens filed against said person(s);
except as herein stated:

Appendix Figure 9 | Affidavit of Seller (continued)

Page 2 of 2   Minnesota Uniform Conveyancing Blanks   Form 50.1.2

4. Any bankruptcy, divorce or dissolution proceeding of record against parties with the same or similar names, during the time period in which the above-named person(s) (has) (have) had any interest in the Premises, are not against the above-named person(s).

5. Any judgments or tax liens of record against parties with the same or similar names are not against the above-named person(s).

6. There has been no labor or materials furnished to the Premises for which payment has not been made.

7. There are no unrecorded contracts, leases, easements, or other agreements or interests relating to the Premises except as stated herein:

8. There are no persons in possession of any portion of the Premises other than pursuant to a recorded document except as stated herein:

9. There are no encroachments or boundary line questions affecting the Premises of which Affiant(s) (has) (have) knowledge.

10. The person(s) (has) (have) not received medical assistance from the State of Minnesota or any county medical assistance agency.

Affiant(s) know(s) the matters herein stated are true and make(s) this Affidavit for the purpose of inducing the acceptance of title to the Premises.

Affiant

_____
(signature)

_____
(signature)

Signed and sworn to before me on _____, by _____
                                        (month/day/year)

_____
                              (insert name of person making statement)

_____.

(Seal, if any)

_____
(signature of notarial officer)

Title (and Rank): _____

My commission expires: _____
                                    (month/day/year)

THIS INSTRUMENT WAS DRAFTED BY:
(insert name and address)

glossary

abstract or **abstract of title** A condensed history or summary of all recorded documents affecting title to a particular tract of land. Most often in form of a book.

abstractor An individual familiar with the filing systems and retrieval of recorded land documents, tax information, and so on. Often used synonymously with "searcher."

access The right to enter and leave a tract of land from a public way, or lands of another.

acknowledgment The act by which a party executing a legal document goes before an authorized officer or notary public and declares the same to be his or her voluntary act or deed.

actual notice Information that can be observed, heard, or otherwise sensed.

administrator A person appointed by a probate court to settle the affairs of a deceased person.

agent Any relationship in which a party (agent) acts for or represents another (principal) under the authority of the latter. Title agents sell policies of a title underwriter, who actually holds reserves to pay title losses.

affidavit A written statement made under oath. A person who lies under oath is subject to penalty and recourse in a court of law.

aka Abbreviation for "also known as."

alienation Transfer, as in transfer of title.

ALTA The American Land Title Association is a trade organization of title insurers, abstractors, title searchers, and other interested parties. They maintain standard forms used commonly in the primary and secondary markets.

alternative title products A series of recently introduced products that use little or no title research but rather substitute risk underwriting, credit scores, or cursory title checks in place of title insurance. No protection is offered for an owner under these products, and, in some states, they have been determined as illegal.

appurtenance Anything that is automatically transferred with the land, including fixtures, improvements, and rights, that routinely go with the land, or "run with the land" unless specifically severed.

assessment A local tax levied against a property for a specific purpose, such as a sewer or street lights. May also be referred to as a special, levied, or pending assessment.

assessment rolls The public record of taxable property.

assessor A public official who establishes the value of a property for purposes of taxation.

asset Anything with a dollar value that you own.

assignee One to whom a transfer of interest is made. For example, the assignee of a mortgage or contract may not be the original person that signed the documents but is now receiving the benefit of those documents. For example, Mortgage Company A originated the loan and assigned it to Mortgage Company B so Company B receives the payments.

assignment The transfer of a mortgage or other instrument from one individual or entity to another.

assignor One who makes an assignment. Mortgage Company A in the example above is *assignee*.

attorney in fact One who holds a power of attorney from another allowing him or her to execute a legal document, such as a deed, mortgage, and so on, on behalf of the grantor.

auditor A public official who maintains records on assessments, delinquent taxes, and so on.

avulsion A sudden loss of land due to natural forces, such as washing away of shore. Often the result of a flood, earthquake, and so on.

bankrupt A person who, through a court proceeding, is relieved from the payment of debts after surrender of all his or her assets to a court appointed trustee.

beneficiary One for whose benefit a trust is created.

Blackacre or **Black Acre** A generic name for a parcel of land. John Doe is to any person as Blackacre is to any piece of land.

blanket easement An easement covering a large portion of land that is not defined as to location or width. In some locations a blanket easement is considered a title problem, in others, customary.

block An area of land within a subdivision that has been surveyed and platted, most often containing lots or outlots.

boilerplate The preprinted part of a form that is the same for all properties; for example, a FNMA mortgage where the language is standard for all loans, except the fill-ins.

book and page The location of a recorded document in an office of records referenced by separate book number and page number, and within that book, documents are listed chronologically and alphanumerically. Now frequently replaced by document number or official record.

bundle of rights A framework designed to help understand the concept of liens, encumbrances, and rights in title to real estate, and how they are separate but interrelate. Individual rights are often referred to as "sticks" in the bundle.

captive reinsurance The illegal practice of setting up a title agency with a lender, builder, or real estate company for the express purpose of kickback money in exchange for business.

caveat Latin for "beware," that is, "watch out" for this!

chain (1) A chronological list of previous owners and encumbrances on a parcel of land. (2) A unit of measurement equaling 66 feet, or 4 Rods.

chattels Another name for personal property (i.e., all property except real property).

clear title (aka marketable title) Ownership where all liens, liabilities, or charges upon a parcel of land have been identified and are understood, so that title is acceptable for purchase. (You know where all the "sticks" are in the bundle of rights.)

closer An attorney or other person responsible for orchestrating a closing, often including drafting legal documents, receipting and explaining documents, handling funds, and meeting terms of the purchase agreement, lender requirements, and title company.

closing The consummation of a real estate sale, where funds change hands, and property is legally transferred. Also called "settlement."

closing in escrow The receiving of all funds and documents to complete the terms of a sale, at which time proceeds are disbursed.

closing protection letter (aka insured closing letter) A letter issued by a title underwriter, accepting responsibility for certain closing (nontitle) issues.

cloud on title Any document, claim, unreleased lien, or encumbrance that may superficially impair or injure the title to a property or cast doubt on the title's validity.

coinsurance Risk divided equally among two or more underwriters at the onset of a transaction—each picks up their respective half, one-third, and so on.

collateral An asset (such as a home) that can be used to secure the repayment of a debt. The borrower risks losing that asset if the loan is not repaid in a timely fashion. Real estate is used as collateral for a mortgage debt. Mortgages are used as collateral for securities.

commitment Preliminary report issued before the actual policy, showing the condition of the title and steps necessary to clear and to transfer title. An offer to insure.

common elements Shared interests among owners where property is used in common with others, such as in town house developments, condominiums, and so on.

common interest community (cic) Property that has certain shared characteristics such as driveways, common walls, parks, and so on. Identified by a declaration of covenants filed on the property and conditions and restrictions on the title.

conditions Additional information that must be supplied to an underwriter before a title policy will be issued free of an exception to the title policy; also, the section of a title policy that outlines the contractual relationship between the insurance company and the insured.

condominium A building in which each unit owner has title to a specific air space unit. The owners may also have the exclusive use of certain limited common areas. Identified by a declaration of covenants filed on the property that identifies covenants, conditions, and restrictions and sets forth the condominium designation.

construction loan or interim loan A loan to provide the funds necessary to pay for the construction of buildings or homes. The lender or title company advances funds to the builder at periodic intervals as the work progresses.

constructive notice Notice given to the world by recorded documents. People are charged with knowledge of recorded documents under the law.

contract for deed (aka land contract) An agreement to sell and purchase under which the legal title is withheld from the purchaser until such time as the required payments to the seller have been completed.

convey The act of deeding or transferring title to another; alienation of title.

conveyance An instrument that transfers title to a property such as a deed.

cooperative Ownership by an association that in turn leases to tenants who are members in the cooperative association.

covenants, conditions, and restrictions (CC&Rs) Legally enforceable limitations on the use of land.

covered risks Risks covered by the policy.

dba Abbreviation for "doing business as."

decree of distribution The final declaration of the rights of heirs to receive the property of an estate.

dedication (1) The giving of streets and easements to a city, township, and so on, on a subdivision plat. (2) The written portion of a plat that describes the plat's legal name, the lots, blocks, outlots, names of streets, ways, roads, easements, and so on. (3) The giving by an owner of private property for public use. (4) The acceptance by the proper public authority of public land.

deed A written document by which title to land is transferred to another, if valid legal requirements are met.

deed of trust Financing instrument that gives a legal claim to a trustee, who may foreclose in the event of default by the borrower.

defalcation The act of embezzling, stealing, or diverting funds, typically occurring during a closing when funds are being handled and exchanged by the closer.

default The omission or failure to perform a legal duty or obligation.

defeasible Title that can be "defeated" due to a deed restriction or forfeiture provision.

dissolution A legal cancellation or annulment of a contract, a business association, such as a partnership or corporation, or a marriage.

document number The identifying number assigned to a document by the local recording agency's office, which directs you to the complete document. It may be expressed as book and page, docket and page, liber and page, official record, or a simple chronological number.

duty to defend A clause in the title policy whereby the underwriter is required to defend *any* attack on the title at no cost to the policy holder.

earnest money Advance payment of part of the purchase price to bind a contract to purchase property.

easement An interest in land, owned by another, that entitles its holder to a specific limited use, such as laying a sewer, installing power or telephone lines, or crossing property.

effective date A "snapshot in time" showing the status in title at a certain moment through which all recorded documents have been searched.

egress The right of exit from a property.

eminent domain The government's right to take property, with just compensation, when for the public good.

encroachment An improvement, such as a house, wall, fence, or garage, that illegally intrudes upon another's real property (includes subsurface, surface, and air rights).

encumbrance Any burden or charge against the title, such as a mortgage, restriction, or easement.

endorsement An amendment to an insurance contract altering its coverage or scope of coverage.

escheat The government's right to take property when someone dies with no will and no heirs.

estate A person's possessions, both real and personal.

examination of title The interpretation of the record title to real property based on a thorough search of public records and other information, to determine ownership, liens, and encumbrances.

exceptions to coverage Items that are not covered by a title policy such as recorded encumbrances. They are specifically outlined in the title commitment and title policy.

exclusions to coverage A list of items shown on the title policy that are not covered by the title policy and are general to all properties. They are shown on the title policy cover.

Expanded Coverage Residential Loan Policy ALTA's new loan policy as of January 1, 2008.

extended coverage When standard exceptions are deleted.

fee simple estate The greatest private interest in a parcel of land that is possible to own. Sometimes stated as "fee simple absolute."

filing A system of legal recording where the court or office maintains the original document, as in district court proceedings or makes a record of such document. In some locales, used interchangeably with "recording."

financing statement A document encumbering personal property or fixtures with debt. A uniform commercial code (UCC) conveyance.

fixture Personal property so attached to real estate, by intent, that it becomes real property (e.g., plumbing fixtures, electrical fixtures, heating fixtures, etc.).

fka Abbreviation for "formerly known as."

foreclosure A proceeding in or out of court, to extinguish all rights, title, and interest of the owner of a property to satisfy a debt.

forfeiture clause A reversionary statement that could cause loss of the property.

gap (1) The period of time between which a search has been done of the public record and the current date. (2) A sliver of land between two other parcels.

general lien A lien filed against the name of an individual, corporation, and so on, that attaches to all properties owned by the individual, both real and personal.

geocode "Smart" numbers used to identify the specific geographical location of a property such as the section, township, and range numbers. Often used in tax parcel identification.

government rights The category of rights including eminent domain, escheat, police powers, and taxation that are always unavailable to an individual.

grantee A person who receives an interest in land by a written instrument.

grantor A person who transfers by a written instrument, an interest in land.

grantor/grantee index Found in most counties, the official records used to identify documents filed on real estate, using names of the grantors and grantees.

habendum clause The "to have and to hold" clause in a legal document that defines the extent of the estate being conveyed (a life estate, an easement, for ten years, forever, subject to certain rights, etc.).

heir One who might inherit or succeed to an interest in lands under the rules of law that apply where an individual dies that has an interest in said land.

hereditaments Inheritable rights.

Homeowner's Policy of Title Insurance ALTA's title insurance policy for one- to four-family residences.

homestead (1) Property tax homestead—A tax classification for a personal residence, allowing a discount on real estate taxes. (2) Legal homestead—A right that allows a property to be exempt from certain judgments and taxes. Legal homestead is proved through a court order called a "declaratory judgment."

HUD-1 The U.S. Department of Housing and Urban Development Settlement Statement.

impact fee A fee imposed on a new development to help pay for the community's cost of providing services.

improvements Those additions to land, made with the intent of being permanent, and tending to increase value, such as buildings, fixtures, streets, sewers, landscaping, and so on.

indemnify To agree to make payments for a loss. Title insurance indemnifies owners and lenders.

ingress The right to enter upon a property.

instrument Any writing having legal form and significance, such as a deed, mortgage, will, lease, and so on. Instrument is used interchangeably with the words "document" and "record."

insure To indemnify against loss or damage.

insure over To give special coverage for a known problem. It does not make the problem go away, but provides for monetary compensation if a problem occurs.

insured closing letter A letter issued by a title underwriter to a lender or buyer accepting responsibility for certain closing (nontitle) issues.

insuring provisions An outline in the title policy explaining what coverage is being given to an insured.

intestate Without a last will and testament.

joint tenancy Two or more people holding title to real estate jointly for life; the survivor(s) taking the interest of the other owner(s) upon their death.

judgment A decree of the court. In practice this is the lien or charge affecting property of a debtor resulting from the court's award of money to a creditor.

junior lien Any lien or mortgage that has less priority than another. May be a judgment or a second or third mortgage filed after another lien.

lease A grant of the use of land and/or land improvements for a specific length of time in consideration for the payment of rent.

leasehold estate The right of a tenant to possession of real estate during the term of the lease.

legal description A description of a tract of land in legally acceptable terms, intended to show the location and dimensions of a piece of property to such a degree that a surveyor can locate it on the ground. Typically described as: section, township, and range; metes and bounds; or lot, block, and subdivision.

lessee One who rents land on a lease.

lessor One who grants the use of lands under the terms of a lease.

letters testamentary Order of a probate court granting authority to the personal representative of an estate.

lien A dollar claim upon a piece of property for the payment or satisfaction of a debt or obligation. Examples are mortgage liens, judgment liens, and mechanics' liens.

lien waiver A document provided by a contractor, subcontractor, or materialman, showing that they have been paid for their work and are waiving rights to file a lien.

life estate The right of use, occupancy, and ownership for the life of an individual.

life tenant The owner of a life estate.

limited common elements A space designated in a condominium or other shared use real estate that has been designated on the plat as for the use of one particular unit.

lis pendens Latin, "pending litigation." A notice recorded to indicate that a lawsuit is pending affecting the lands where the notice is recorded.

marketable title A "good" title, one where there is no reasonable doubt as to the interests held in land; one that can be readily transferred to another party.

mechanic's lien A lien allowed by statute for an amount owed to contractors, laborers, and suppliers of materials to buildings or other structures where work was performed or materials supplied for the improvement of the land.

metes-and-bounds description A description of land by measures and distances. It must have a known point of beginning, define the perimeter of a parcel, and return to the point of beginning to be legally acceptable.

mortgage A document used to encumber real estate as a security for repayment of a debt.

mortgagee A designation for the mortgage lender.

mortgage note A negotiable (transferable to a third party) instrument used in conjunction with a mortgage that outlines the terms of the mortgage and promises to repay the debt.

mortgage registration tax (MRT) A tax charged by some states to record a mortgage deed. It is based on the value of the mortgage as spelled out on the mortgage deed. It is most often paid by the borrower in the transaction.

mortgagor A designation for the mortgage borrower.

name searches Searches made by an abstractor or technical searcher for general liens filed against a person's name, such as state and federal tax liens, bankruptcies, judgments, probate liens, and so on.

nka Abbreviation for "now known as."

notary or notary public A person legally authorized to administer oaths and take acknowledgments that legally attest to the authenticity of signatures.

notice of lis pendens A document filed to show that there is pending litigation against the real estate.

novation The legal substitution of one party for another under the terms of a mortgage note and mortgage deed or deed of trust. Releases liability of the original mortgagor and substitutes liability of the person assuming the loan.

owner and encumbrance (O&E) report A property report prepared by abstractors or searchers that provides summarized and *incomplete* information on a given parcel of land, generally including the last owner of record and recent liens.

ownership The right to possess and use property to the exclusion of others; title.

parcel map A map of a given area, designed, drawn, and labeled for the purposes of identifying parcels and distinguishing them from one another in a given area. Sometimes known as a subdivision map or a plat map.

partition (1) Division by the court system separating land into specific parcels among parties who are in dispute as to ownership and or use (partition by kind). (2) A forced sale by the court, who distributes the sale proceeds among the owners (partition by sale).

patent Original conveyance from the U.S. government to an individual or state.

personal property Chattels. All property that is not real estate, including monies, contracts, mortgages, automobiles, jewelry, and so on.

personal representative A person appointed by court to carry out the terms of a will or administer the estate of a decedent who died without a will.

plat (1) A recorded map representing a piece of land subdivided into lots and blocks. Upon recording, and if complete, it may transfer title to roads, streets, alleys, and so on, to the public, and will create easements or restrictions when shown in the document. (2) A sketch of a parcel of property showing locations of easements and improvements.

plat book Identifies the location of all land in a county by section/township/range or by subdivision lot-and-block numbers. Plat books sometimes show name of owner, the road on which parcel is located, number of acres or dimensions of tract or lot, and so on, as of a certain point in time.

point of beginning The origination and destination of a metes and bounds legal description.

police powers The right of the government to enforce laws for public welfare, including such things as health issues, building codes, zoning, and so on.

power of attorney (POA) A document authorizing another person to act on his or her behalf as his or her agent or attorney. Often used to sign deeds or mortgages in the buyers' or sellers' absence with their legally executed POA document.

premium Fee paid to purchase insurance.

primary mortgage market Originators of mortgages, who generally sell them to the secondary market.

probate (1) Legal proceeding to distribute the assets of an estate. (2) Any action over which a probate court has jurisdiction.

probate court A court having jurisdiction over real and personal property, whether of a deceased, minor, or an incompetent person.

public land survey system (PLSS) A U.S. government mapping plan, using a system of one-mile sections within townships and ranges, and covering about 72 percent of U.S. lands.

purchase-money mortgage A mortgage given as part of the buyer's consideration for the purchase of real property and delivered at the same time that the real property is transferred as a simultaneous part of the transaction.

quiet title/quiet title action/quiet title suit An action in court that produces a final determination of the rights of parties who are in dispute over real estate.

quitclaim deed A deed intended to pass any title, interest, or claim that the grantor may have in the property but not containing any warranty of a valid interest or title in the grantor.

real property Land, including surface, subsurface, and air rights, along with improvements to the land, and the rights, title, and interests that go with the land.

recital A reference within a document, providing legal notice (constructive notice) of certain rights or reservations.

record or official record The International Organization for Standardization defines a record as "information created, received, and maintained as evidence and information by an organization, or person, in pursuance of legal obligations or in the transaction of business."

recorder A public official who is charged with maintaining the official land record system, along with various liens, encumbrances, and so on.

recording The filing and indexing of documents affecting real property to make them public record and give public notice to all future purchasers, creditors, or other interested parties.

rectangular survey system Another name for the public land survey system. A method using sections, townships, and ranges, quarter sections, and so on, to describe the location of a parcel of land.

reinsurance Ceding off a portion of insurance risk to one or more companies, known as "reinsurers," in order to limit risk.

release An instrument relinquishing the hold on a previously established claim against property. Most commonly used as a release of lien or release of mortgage where the debt has been satisfied or forgiven.

reliction The exposing of land due to natural forces of waters receding.

remainderman The person receiving title upon the death of a life tenant.

re-recording The recording of a deed for the second time to correct an error contained in the deed when originally recorded. Also called "corrective deed" or "reformation deed."

reversioner The person to whom title is returned upon the death of a life tenant.

right of first refusal The right of a person to have the first opportunity to either purchase or lease real property.

riparian rights Rights of a land owner whose property is bounded by non-navigable waters to the reasonable use of the water or waterbed for such things as boating, fishing, recreation, swimming, drawing water, bathing, and so on.

satisfaction of mortgage The document issued by the mortgagee when the mortgage loan is paid in full. Also called a "release of mortgage."

Schedule A Precise information about the specific transaction used for closing and to create legal documents.

Schedule B List of all title issues pertaining to the property being insured.

secondary mortgage market The market in which primary mortgage lenders sell mortgages to obtain more funds in order to originate more new loans. The sale of mortgages by the primary market provides liquidity for them.

second mortgage A mortgage recorded subsequent to another mortgage and subordinate to the first one.

security interest An interest that one takes in the borrower's property to assure repayment of a debt, including: a mortgage; a vendor's interest in a contract for deed or land contract; a deed given as security for a debt; a lessor's interest in a lease; a holder of a sheriff's certificate during the redemption period; an assignee's interest in an assignment of leases or rents; and so on.

specific lien A lien filed against a specific piece of real estate that does not impact other real estate or personal property of the lienee. Examples: a mortgage/deed of trust, mechanics' liens.

standard exceptions Exceptions to title that appear on all title commitments and policies, unless they are disposed of to the satisfaction of the title company.

standard policy Policy usually used for commercial properties and corporations.

state deed tax A tax required by the state to record a deed, based on sale price.

subrogation The giving of legal rights from the owner/lender to the title company to defend title, "allowing another to stand in your shoes." This prevents the insured from collecting both from the title company and again from the party causing the loss, and it allows the title company to attempt to recoup money on their own behalf.

sworn construction statement A document completed and signed by the contractor on a newly built or remodeled home that lists all of the costs, subcontractors, and materials and suppliers. Lien waivers provided by the material suppliers and laborers are attached as proof of payment.

table funding Closing that buyers, sellers, and interested parties attend to sign documents and exchange funds at one time (prior to recording).

taxation The government's right to charge fees on property to gain revenue. They can take title to property if taxes are not paid.

tenancy in common An estate or interest in land held by two or more persons, each having equal rights of possession and enjoyment, but no right of survivorship.

testament The document describing the wishes of a person upon death. Also referred to as "last will and testament."

testate Having a last will and testament.

title (1) The evidence of rights that a person has to the ownership and possession of land. (2) Ownership itself.

title agent A representative of a title underwriter, one who "writes" the policies of the actual insurer or underwriter.

title assurance Evidence pertaining to title. It can take on many forms: abstracts of title, Torrens certificates of title, attorneys' opinions about title, surveys, title insurance, and so on.

title binder The commitment to insure.

title commitment A document that reflects all of the title research done on property. Its purpose is to inform all parties of any encumbrances affecting the property and to commit to insure property, subject to certain stated requirements. Also known as a title binder.

title defect (1) Title that lacks some of the necessary elements to transfer "good and marketable title." (2) Impaired ownership or marketability of real estate title, sometimes referred to as "cloud on title."

title insurance A policy of indemnity issued by a title insurance underwriter or its agent that insures a buyer or lender against monetary loss or damage due to errors in the title as described in the policy and undeterminable factors that affect title such as fraud, forgery, unrecorded documents, unknown heirs, and many other factors.

title plant Records kept by title companies of public recordings that affect title to real estate, such as deeds, mortgages, easements, judgments, bankruptcies, and so on.

title policy The actual document that creates liability on behalf of the title insurer.

title search An examination of public records to determine the legal ownership of property. Usually performed by an attorney, abstractor, skilled title searcher, or title company.

Title Standards General "rules of thumb" as set out by various bar associations as to the acceptability of what is considered "marketable title."

title underwriter The title insurer who holds a statutory premium reserve and is responsible for claims on title under a title insurance policy.

tract (1) Generally, an area of land. (2) In the U.S. public land survey system, an area of four townships by four townships, where correction lines are made along the northerly and westerly most lines thereof.

tract check A request, usually just prior to closing, to determine if anything has been filed against a property between the effective date of the commitment and closing (aka the gap period) that might prevent successful transfer of the title. Also known as an update or downdate.

tract index In many counties, a geographic index used to locate documents filed on a particular piece of property.

treasurer The public official charged with the collection of real estate taxes and other monetary duties.

trust (1) A right of property held by one for the benefit of another. (2) A document defining the terms of a fiduciary responsibility where property has been conveyed for someone's benefit.

trustee A person who holds a property in trust.

trustor A person who places property into a trust.

underwriter (1) The actual company that holds reserves to pay losses on title policies, as opposed to an agent, who sells the policies of the underwriter. (2) Person responsible for evaluating risk of title defects and determining conditions to the commitment to insure.

underwriting Deciding whether to make a commitment to insure a potential buyer based on certainty of title, age of any defects in title, and other risk factors with the matching of risk to an appropriate rate risk or subject to certain conditions.

underwriting manual A text given to title agents and employees of a title underwriter to assist in resolving common title issues, give company policy, and provide standard language for use in title commitments and policies.

vault exam An examination of title to a piece of real estate without benefit of an abstract through reviewing the public records or title plant records directly. Often done in the Northeast.

vendee A purchaser of real property, generally under a purchase agreement or contract for deed (aka land contract).

vendor A seller of real property generally under a purchase agreement or contract for deed (aka land contract).

warranty deed A deed intended to pass any title, interest, or claim that the grantor may have in the property, and containing a warranty of a valid interest or title in the grantor.

warranty of title An agreement and assurance by the grantor of real property for himself or herself and his or her heirs, to the effect that he or she is the owner and has the right to sell or encumber.

will A written document providing for the distribution of property owned by a deceased person.

answer key

Chapter 1

Case Study

1. Pam is the life tenant pur autre vie (for the life of Charles's mother).
2. Charles is the grantor.
3. St. Andrew's Church is the remainderman.
4. Reversioner is the term used for Charles if the property returned in fee to Charles on his mother's death.
5. Yes, the life estate is an insurable estate for the life tenant. However, lenders are often unwilling to lend money to a life tenant, because the lender's security would terminate on the untimely death of the life tenant. To resolve this, they would ask for the remainderman to sign the mortgage as well.

Review Questions

1. **d.** Knowing the status of title making sure unwanted liens are paid and protecting oneself are all good motives for purchasing title insurance.
2. **b.** Title insurance is monetary indemnity that the insured will receive compensation for loss.
3. **d.** Encroachments are illegal overlaps onto another's property, not rights.
4. **a.** Contracts are personal property.
5. **b.** Personal property is most often sold by a bill of sale. It is mortgaged by a UCC.
6. **b.** Emblements are personal property, an exception to the rule.
7. **a.** Personal property is to a UCC what real property is to a mortgage.
8. **d.** Real estate taxes are always considered a "first lien" on real estate.
9. **d.** Escheat is the government's right to take real or personal property when a person dies with no heirs or a will.
10. **d.** Rights of the government exist in the following order (highest priority to lowest): federal, state, county, city.

Chapter 2

Case Study

1. **c.** Acme Title Company is responsible to clear the closing error because it listed the wrong loan number, causing someone else's loan to be paid off.
2. **d.** Tom could have helped Susan by requesting a closing protection letter from the title underwriter.

Review Questions

1. **b.** An unsigned deed provides no assurance.
2. **a.** Title insurance protects real estate agents by providing access to professionals to help the title problems.

3. **a.** Title policies legally indemnify the insured against title issues, not closing issues.
4. **a.** Bond employees handle large sums of money.
5. **d.** Mortgage money is funded by the primary market and the secondary market.
6. **c.** The primary market originates loans directly to the consumer.
7. **d.** All functions of title companies listed assist the secondary market.
8. **a.** A commitment is also known as a title binder.
9. **b.** An insured closing letter does not assume risk for failure of banks through which funds are drawn to be solvent.
10. **d.** *Defalcation* refers to the fact that funds have been stolen.

Chapter 3

Case Study

Following are some points for the buyer to consider when making a decision on an owner's title policy.

- The title insurance company will lay out a complete look at the title, including tax information, the size and location of easements, outstanding mortgages, and any restrictive covenants that the buyer needs to be aware of.
- The cost of the policy in relation to the home is minimal and the premium is paid only once, while the coverage continues until she sells and even into the future if she sells by warranty deed.
- The recent work done to the property by the sellers is a $30,000 risk to the buyer because it is a lien against the property. The only way to ensure that she will not suffer a loss due to unpaid contractors or subcontractors is to buy an owner's policy covering that threat.
- There are numerous judgments against the uncle's name, which adds risk to the policy. Because it is a common name, we do not know if the uncle is the same person against whom the judgments are filed. If he is, the judgments are a lien on the property. It is particularly difficult because the sellers are unable to give an affidavit stating the judgments are not against the uncle. The buyer should discuss this problem with the title company to ensure that her policy will cover that problem.
- Because the sellers will not give a warranty deed on the property, the buyer has no recourse against the sellers for any title problems.

Review Questions

1. **d.** Twenty-five percent of files have title defects.
2. **d.** Title insurance cannot guarantee that a person can retain title and possession of property under any circumstances. If fraud, forgery, or unrecorded but valid documents are disclosed, a person may lose title and possession, but will obtain monetary remuneration.
3. **d.** Title insurers assume the monetary risk from the insured.
4. **d.** The best title examination cannot detect fraud, a forged signature, or an unrecorded document.
5. **c.** An estimated 40 percent of U.S. homeowners do not have an owner's title policy.
6. **c.** A mortgage policy is most likely to decrease in value over time.
7. **a.** An owner's policy is *NOT* assignable.

8. **d.** An owner's title policy provides a contractual duty to defend all claims covered under the policy.
9. **b.** Title premiums are a reasonable buy in a claims-filled environment.
10. **a.** Title underwriters and agents suffer from the volatility of a fluctuating market.

Chapter 4

Case Study

Items 1, 2, and 3. These are likely no surprise and will be handled according to the purchase agreement.

Item 4. You will want to determine what the pending improvement is for and the anticipated cost and date of the improvement.

Item 6. You will want to determine where the easements are located. This will likely require a survey and will be critical to the placement of any buildings.

Item 7. You will want to determine the terms of the developer's agreement. A copy will need to be obtained and reviewed. Also, if the impact fee was not anticipated, decisions will need to be made about how it is handled between the buyers and sellers.

Item 8. What do the restrictions say? A copy will need to be obtained and reviewed.

Item 9. Is John Banks the same person as the judgment debtor? If he is, the judgment will need to be paid. If not, an affidavit of nonidentity will be needed.

Discussion Questions

1. Items 4, 5, 7, 8, and 9 need additional research before the closing.
2. Title work provides *no* information on building codes. These are government rights that fall under the general category of police powers and are exceptions to the title work. The building code information needed should be obtained from the local city or county authority.
3. Title work provides no information on zoning rules. Again, these are government rights that fall under the general category of police powers. Zoning information needs to be obtained from the local city or county authority. In a transaction this large, however, an endorsement to a title policy may be negotiated to ensure Mr. Gates can build under the current zoning rules.

Review Questions

1. **d.** The commitment reflects all of the title research done and is used to prepare closing documents.
2. **a.** Schedule A shows the effective date, how sellers currently hold title, and a precise legal description.
3. **b.** Schedule B contains exclusions specific to the property.
4. **b.** The commitment is generally good for only 60 days, after which it expires.
5. **c.** Encroachments are exceptions to coverage that you will rarely find on title commitments.
6. **a.** Utility and drainage are the most common easements found on properties.

7. **c.** *Home equity line of credit* is a term often used by bankers when loaning money secured by a home (i.e., a second mortgage).
8. **a.** Bankruptcy is a court proceeding relieving someone from payment of his or her debts.
9. **a.** Cloud on title is a generic term referring to impaired marketability.
10. **d.** An affidavit of nonidentity is most frequently used as a tool so that judgments are not required to be paid at closing.
11. **d.** Eminent domain is the government right used when property is needed for the public good.
12. **d.** Notice of lis pendens means pending litigation.

Chapter 5

Case Study

1. **b.** The extended policy coverage that insured the encroachment of the house onto the five-foot utility easement is survey.
2. **b.** The extended policy coverage that insured the problem of needing to purchase two and one half feet of Henry's property is survey.
3. **a.** Probate of Henry's estate to buy the land was covered by the title policy.
4. **a.** True
5. **a.** True

Review Questions

1. **c.** Covered risks insure that a legal right of access to and from the land exists.
2. **c.** Conditions outline the contractual relationships.
3. **b.** Exclusions are shown in a list of items on the policy jacket.
4. **d.** Schedule A states what and who are being insured and the type of policy.
5. **a.** Schedule A describes the name of the insured and policy amount.
6. **b.** Government rights fall under the exclusions section.
7. **d.** Schedules A and B show the specifics of the particular parcel, the meat of the policy.
8. **d.** Endorsements modify a policy or commitment.
9. **a.** Covered risks assure title to the estate or interest described in Schedule A.
10. **a.** There are no liens or encumbrances on the title except as shown in the policy. (Policies insure that there is *legal* access to and from the land. They cannot insure that you will not lose possession, because documents in the chain may be forged, or unrecorded documents may exist.)
11. **a.** True, what one title company refuses to insure, another title company may insure.

Chapter 6

Case Study

1. **d.** Order processing will need to order all new information, including taxes and assessments; the inspector will have to re-inspect the correct property and get a survey or plat; the title searcher will have to research all new information as to recorded documents and judgment lien searches; the title examiner will have to examine all new documents and prepare a

new title commitment; and the closer will again have to prepare all legal documents and closing statements after obtaining new mortgage payoffs, etc.
2. Because the seller is deceased, probate documents will need to be obtained and reviewed in order to establish the heirs, and who will be deeding out to the buyers.

Review Questions

1. **b, a, d, c**
2. **d, b, c, a**
3. **b.** Call a title examiner/attorney for technical questions about clearing title on a title commitment.
4. **b.** Marketing generally responds to training by customers.
5. **c.** An underwriter determines if sticky title exceptions can be insured over.
6. **d.** Record keeping would have a copy of the HUD-1 closing statement 18 months after the file is closed.
7. **c.** The abstractor/searcher locates judgments and state and federal tax liens in the public record.
8. **d.** Closers/closing attorneys create HUD-1 closing statements.
9. **c.** Closing in escrow is when title agents handle the closing details without meeting the buyers and sellers face to face.
10. **d.** Lenders, closing assistants, and closers all must know the general rules of the VA, FHA, or FHLMC.
11. **c.** The policy is the key document that shows the complete status of title.